PLAIN SONGS

PLAIN SONGS

Stories & Poems

by
Carleton Writers

Clare Rossini
Robert Tisdale
Mary Moore Easter
Sigrun Leonhard
Wayne Carver
Susan Jaret McKinstry
Keith Harrison
Jane Taylor McDonnell
Gregory Blake Smith

Edited by Keith Harrison

A Publication of Carleton College
1990

ISBN   0-9613911-5-4

CONTENTS

ACKNOWLEDGMENTS

This book owes its publication to the generosity and encouragement of a great number of administrators, faculty, students and alumni. We would like to thank, in particular, Dean Elizabeth McKinsey, President Stephen Lewis, Vice President Perry Mason, the Board of Trustees and all those who looked on the idea with a kindly eye.

*

Some of the pieces printed here have appeared, or will appear shortly elsewhere, as follows:

Legs by Keith Harrison in *The Australian* (Sydney) and *Thank You, Pythagoras,* by the same author, in *Overland,* No. 119 (Melbourne).

The following poems by Clare Rossini, some in slightly different versions, appeared in these periodicals: *Portrait: The Adolescent Self* and *Leave of Absence* in *Black Warrior Review; A Mourning Dove in New York City* and *Self Portrait as Woman, Aged Thirty, Posed on Flowered Couch* in *The Kenyon Review; The Absolute* in *Poetry; For a Friend Since Youth* and *After Your Death* in *Poetry Northwest; Scene Between a Mother and Grandmother* and *The Pleasures of Perspective* in *Prairie Schooner.*

Susan Jaret McKinstry's story *Divisions* first appeared in *The Carleton Magazine,* No.1 and the short story *Hands* by Gregory Blake Smith was originally published in *Kenyon Review,* Vol.V, No. 1, Winter 1983.

For permission to reprint these poems and stories we thank the respective editors.

*

Finally, we are most grateful to Melissa Flynn for designing the cover and to Joseph Byrne for permission to reproduce his painting *The Blue House;* to Janet Holmes for her experienced eye; to Liz Lupien for her proofreading, pasting-up and versatile professionalism; to James Shoop, Deborah Blakeley, and Dan Bergeson for their practical suggestions and kindness. We originally thought of calling this book *Nine Hands:* a serious understatement, for without the help of many more than that we would have not have arrived here.

K.H.

FOREWORD

With people like Reed Whittemore, Erling Larsen, Wayne Carver, Arthur Mizener, Scott Elledge, Jack Lucas, and many others, constituting an essential part of Carleton's legacy, it's not surprising that writers who are also teachers are drawn to live and work here. The surprising, and gratifying thing is that we have been, and are surrounded by so many highly productive artists in *other* fields - painters, photographers, dancers, storytellers of all kinds, a jeweller, a composer - as well as performing artists in music and theater.

In this collection we present only nine faculty artists, all of them working mainly in words. But we draw a great deal of nourishment from the fact that interaction between the arts is one of the givens in our life here. Sometimes two artists are combined in one person, as is the case of Mary Moore Easter, who - in the middle of her career as a dancer - began writing poems several years ago, and is now, quite literally, combining poetry and dance in much of her work.

We have also been nourished for years by a sympathetic administration who believe that *doing* is often a very useful complement to teaching, and they have been very quick to support this, and many other projects aimed at making the work of the faculty more available to alumni, students, our colleagues and the general public.

As compiler of this collection, it's been very pleasing to experience the variety of voices and styles in the work of my colleagues, to know that writing is very much alive outside the English Department as well as inside it, and to present, with a solid selection from each, a number of writers who - out of modesty - might be better known as teachers than as practitioners. We hope that this book will, among other things, redress that imbalance, and we hope that it will be followed by further collections which will go some way toward revealing the full range of the imaginative work that is going on within these green and white acres.

Keith Harrison

Carleton College, 1990

CLARE ROSSINI

A MOURNING DOVE IN NEW YORK CITY

Waking, I hear its cryptic trill,
And I'm back twenty years,
In bed at my grandmother's house,
My warmth softening sheets
Scarred by mending.

Downstairs, the clock chimes;
My grandmother's steps begin to trace
The choreography of breakfast-making.
I hear my mother's voice break in,
Her second-generation laughter.

I slip from the bed. The floor is cold,
The stairs down dangerously steep.
I waver at the top of them, adrift
In the scent of coffee...

A renter wakes there this morning.
The china cups: sold. And the clock -
Someone has it who cannot translate
Its hourly lament for the deep,
Aromatic couch, the faint edge
Of lace doily shining.

The cry of the mourning dove rises
Over a small Minnesota town,
Over the prairie churning out wheat
And flowers, over those sheets,
Wherever they are, their stitches still locked
In small, endless embraces,

And wakens me from an older sleep
Desiring to be at table
Between two large, female bodies,
Watching the morning sun
Set dimestore glasses afire.

SELF PORTRAIT AS ADOLESCENT

As I undressed, I sensed
Movement behind me. I turned:
It was my own nakedness
That stalled in the shadows

Cluttering my mirror like leaves.
I stared at this stranger
With breasts tipped out,
Catching the light,

With a narrowing waist,
With a belly taking on
A lower gleam.
In the moment before shame returned,

I admired myself
As if I were
The sentimentalist
Who had sculpted that soft new form -

I stood there,
Flushed
With the pleasure
Of an original--

As if all history had
Flowed back
Into the clean slate of my body;
As if that twilight were the first

Twilight falling, darkening
The unfinished earth,
The polished new
Fathoms of air.

FLESH/SPIRIT

This air that burns between us
Is ordered
Like the atmosphere of heaven,

One rank of angel assigned
To each immaculate zone. And as I move
Closer to you,

It grows seraphic, pitches toward
A soprano hum
That is round and gold as gesture.

So why touch?
Through such Platonic latitudes,
Why move this hand infected

With finity and heat?
Nonetheless,
As I look to where it lies

Half-open in my lap,
I know my hand
Will find its way to you.

It is a gypsy; it knows
The back roads of dusk,
The venial underpasses.

It will come upon you as you sleep,
Rouse you
With a touch at your ear,

Play for you: you, the instrument
That will warm with its
Ethnic music.

Oh my love
It will leave you
Penniless by dawn.

FOR A FRIEND SINCE YOUTH

Sixteen years old and bored,
We damned the world
And at 2 a.m. took
Your slipshod Chevy to the road.

Even at high speed, the air
Flowing through the windows
Seemed calm and sweet
With summer.

As we rounded a curve, laughing,
I imagined a moment
That never came,
The brakes singing
Like crazed seraphim,
Our bodies breaking the windshield
As if it were the surface
Of the smooth black lake we swam in...

How careful we've become
With our lives. Over tea today,
We spoke of the city, glittering,
Dangerous;

Of our nuclear dreams;
Of those cells in your body
The doctors call "precancerous" -
Which you laugh off, your eyes

Still that rare light green,
Your head massed with curls
That once made boys' fingers itch
For new knowledge.

Tonight, 2:03 on my digital,
I'm wakened by an explosion
North of 125th,
The waves of sound washing massively

16

Through our courtyard.
I sit up, panicky
Until your face comes back
As it looked today

When we talked by the fire
Whose flames flushed and dimmed
On your pure cheeks -
You,

My rabbit's foot,
My charm,
You are tinder;
Like the world, you are a perishable

Source of grace,
Still with me as sirens
In the hills of Harlem
Raise and twine their distant keen.

AFTER YOUR DEATH

For awhile I panicked at the ease
With which we left one another, as if those
Who disappeared down our darkening driveways
Would re-emerge from the nothingness
We call late summer. But I've regained
The immunity of the living,
Removed from the rawness of others' griefs,
Sleeping although September's skittish stars
Are falling. Then the light brightens or deepens,
Making a street go strange. Then I turn
To the brief expanse of a human body
Bared for love, yes, even then, and I walk
Towards your young, stilled body again as I
Wildly coerce language into prayer -
As if anything could be heard above
Your incorrigible silence.

GENESIS, AGAIN

Light and dark
Blocked out, a few stars
Set to fall,

Adam and Eve
Still drowsing in blueprint.
Stop it there.

Leave history
Unloosed; beauty,
The trump not laid on the table;

This June
In the wings.
And you, whoever you are -

You impossible, not drafted, not
Your allusive hands, not the largesse
Of your smile.

And I not here either
To claim you
Or to turn away, to continue in either

Tradition of error; not here
To be wakened
By a whispering sound,

And to wonder what it is,
The wind, the snake,
Or merely the slow

Rise and fall
Of your breathing.
This is not the first

Love song, love.
There's been water over the dam,
Heartbreak beyond

That inaugural cleaving,
Loneliness
Deepening like twilight

Across Asia, Europe, America.
Nonetheless,
As the moon drifts up,

Again fills out its
Implacable round,
It comes on with the power

Of the original grief,
This desire
To know you, to honor

The first human vow:
To sleep through the dark hours
Together.

SELF PORTRAIT AS WOMAN, AGED THIRTY, POSED ON FLOWERED COUCH

She thought her education would come
All at once, as it did
For Saul, lucky boy, trailed by lightning

Until the right moment,
Crawling out from under his horse
With a new name and profession.

But daily the weather comes,
And he who claims to love her
Is still there in the morning,

Buttering toast,
Calling her yet
Another nonsensical name.

She imagined the battles of the self
Fought out
In the old high style, leaving her

Dappled with virtue.
But she finds that she's infected
With a mild self-love;

She's the would-be martyr
Who dreams of the executioner's knife
And wakes singing heathen hymns

In her safe bed.
Who will educate her
To the mirror and the clock,

All those exigencies ?
Like a flower,
She colors in the moment.

Meanwhile, the anger of God
Waits in her cupboards,
Ready to fill the house, battering

The knickknacks beyond recognition,
Refounding the Hellenic
Shape she calls fear.

SCENE BETWEEN A MOTHER
AND GRANDMOTHER

There were days when she forgot your name,
Re-made you in the image
Of the friends who used to come
For coffee in her small-town kitchen.
Dorothy, she said as you walked in the room,
Or, *Alice, it's darn good to see you,*
Come in right now out of that cold -

Motioning you to the chair by the lamp,
Dropping stitches in the afghan
Of forgetfulness that filled her lap,
Patterned with bumps and flaring holes,
Drawing together a wild warmth.

One night you found her dressed, packed,
Heading resolutely down the street
Towards the past, insisting she heard
Your childish voice crying for supper.

She struggled with you, pleading
I must get home now, I must get home
To my little girl, her face simplified
In the blue haze of the mercury street lamp
Until you saw your own features in it,
And the pulse surging through your locked hands
Flowed back to your own body, aching

To hold that unappeasable child
Trapped in a fifty-year-old dusk;
Aching to be that child again, and held.

THE PLEASURES OF PERSPECTIVE

(After "Landscape with Castle," Jacob Grimmer, 1592)

Here, at last, a world run by rules.
They insist
That the castle, being closer,
Necessarily dwarfs

The distant, perfect city,
And the foreground's fisherman
(The calm line of his back
Suggesting a fisherman's happiness)

Is the most important of all.
You could linger near the fisher,
Toss stones
Into his black-green lake.

But why not go on?
There are more views
Beyond this one, more sails
Tipped toward home,

And in the overlapping hills,
Spires point to a dozen heavens.
Where the river flows
Into a final mountain,

Where the world
Hones to the vanishing point,
There may be found the room and hour
Where memory begins:

The windows
Transfusing morning light;
The cool floor;
Not even your father risen.

ELEGY FOR A YOUNG ARTIST

for Jennifer Bonner

Purple will miss you.

As will everything you painted
In those wild excursions
That left shoes
Startled into pink,

That brought all you knew
Of green to bear
On one unearthly pineapple,
Much larger than life.

And oh you had style, girl.

At the opening, your skirt
Was short, the color
Of your stockings unreal.
You owned the air,

You raged through it
With the ardor of unspent lightning.
No wonder young men
Dreamed of midnight storms.

No wonder our streetlights
Recall your shape
As do the trees that swayed
Heavily over you, sighing.

Like them, we remember you

In motion:
A blur of red
Biking across campus. A laugh
Floating up a stairwell.

A hand turning the volume up
So the house shook as you
Painted your way
Beyond respirators, blazing lights,

Emergency measures ...
Still it seems,
It will always seem
That you were just here, singing

At the top of your voice.

Now you have become
A public possession, like the sun
Shifting on the Cannon River,
The clearings in the local arboretum,

The stars and the untouched
Spaces between them
Where nightly, silence accrues.
Nothing can take you from us,

No, you are ours now and forever
Free of us -
Like a flame loosened from its wick,
Allowed at last to feed

On a universe of air.

LEAVE OF ABSENCE

Today it seems
Preposterous
To have hauled it this far,
This heart -

Like Hannibal
Going over the Alps -
Wasn't there a way to do
With less baggage?

These views, thank goodness,
Are working their tonic;
These strangers bring back
The pleasures of strangeness.

And after all those months,
Those relentless Novembers,
The afternoon sun pours down
So abundantly

That voices expire
Mid-air,
Gestures fall at my feet,

Unnoticed.
I'm still trying to take in
The sight of the bird bath
Sunk at an angle
At the edge of the yard.

It needs cleaning.
But look how the wind
Troubles the water
To a superficial beauty,

How it then
Calms and clears.
See those shadows at the bottom,
How they shine now,

Now shift,
Now grow utterly
Still -
Like the mind at work in the world.

* * *

I grew up in a family of eight children, and to some extent, my attraction to the penetrating voice of lyric poetry was a defensive measure: I wanted to be heard. Perhaps it's no wonder that my early work was, well, shrill. In eighth grade I produced what I felt was my first Great Work: "And Live, People." Here is its first stanza:

Crawl out of your encompassing shell;
Draw in the fiery breath of life;
Go smell the roses: war is hell!
And live, people.

I was especially proud of my bold use of the expletive: a venial sin, according to the rather exact measure of my Catholic conscience. So I sacrificed my soul for making what I thought was a bold political statement; it didn't occur to me that the cliche was the greatest offense of all.

When I was fifteen, I had the good fortune of taking a poetry-writing course for high school students offered on a local college campus. We read a hodgepodge of twentieth-century poets - Yeats, Rilke, Lowell, Plath, Bishop, Ginsberg, Berryman - and in six weeks, my naive Renaissance sensibility, (see tetrameter, above) was transformed into one which was equally naive, but thoroughly post-modern. Our teachers gave us a long rope: we wrote in every sort of form, including free verse; kept Jungian dream journals; peeled oranges for hours - then wrote haiku about the experience. And we talked about each others' poems, endlessly.

In fact - and now I shall leave that fifteen-year-old with half-peeled orange and make a large leap into the present - I believe that I have learned more about teaching from the creative writing courses that I have taken than from any others. Which is not to say that such courses are always ably taught or that they make ordinary people into "Writers" - heaven forbid! I'm thinking more of the methodology often used in such classes, one which has much to recommend it. Without exception, the creative writing courses I have taken were structured as workshops: that is, writing by class members is distributed in advance, and every student comes to class prepared to offer comments and suggestions. In such courses, the teacher is less a final and dominant authority than a facilitator, a role I'm most comfortable with in my classes. In the best workshops, the historical context, political implications, and above all, the meaning of poems or stories are passionately discussed because workshop students are acutely aware of their responsibility for saying useful, thoughtful things. The writer, after all, is there in the classroom, gulping coffee nervously.

Rilke said that poems must be written out of a sense of necessity, and I feel that teaching - in my case, the teaching of literature - should have the same source. The challenge is to make students approach the text on the page muttering "We've got a live one here," to see themselves as being vitally involved in the formation or reformation of a literary tradition. The questions that arise in creative-writing workshops - "What's this about? What's new, valid, important, imperfect, brilliantly quirky here?" - are questions all readers should ask of all texts, whether or not the writer is in the room. I don't believe in the ivory tower, and as a result, I do believe that good teaching, like good writing, is clearly connected to the lives we draft, edit, revise, and amend on a daily basis.

Clare Rossini

ROBERT TISDALE

FARM DOG

I think the visit was meant to teach me something -
maybe "real life," maybe just horses and cows.
I don't know. What I saw was loutish, turgid, mean.

Huge dray horses with haunches
like Gargantuan hams,
cows with hind quarters, when they walked,
like two ambling ladders under a tent.
A sow and her shoats lay amid flies,
food and shit intermingled,
cabbage stalks and half-gone potatoes
littered about.

The girl explained chickens -
how they peck the weakest to death -
and turkeys so stupid they drown in the rain,
forgetting to shut their mouths.
How tractors break down in the fields
and a man lost his arm in a combine.
When I saw the thresher's long take-off belt
I imagined it loose, flaying a farmboy's back
raw in one terrible blow.

The two-o'clock sun cooked me crazy.
My red skin got dry.
When we played two-person crack-the-whip,
the yard next the house spun and reeled.
I ate dirt and didn't mind.

When it was my turn as center and pivot,
her dog appeared - a German shepherd,
all black and tan. The clear golden eyes,
sleek snout, powerful jaws,
clean white saber teeth sheathed
between silky black lips.
A hundred-ten pounds of fur, muscle, and bone -
lord of the farm, the only aristocrat there.

He looked me over, I repeated his name,
and his muscular tongue licked
my shy hand. Satisfied,
he left for the cool of the barn,
and we started the game over again.

I grabbed her hand and swung her around.
He ran through the yard. From ten feet away
he leapt into the air and hit my chest
like a toppling bale of hay,
slammed me into the dust,
and his teeth pierced my arm like gruyere.

I couldn't believe it. The farm upside down,
the sun kept me still.
There were only her cries and my shock.

Then quickly they whipped back the dog
as I screamed at them all
"Don't hurt him. It was my fault!"
I didn't bleed much or pass out.
They didn't shoot him.
Tetanus shots and stitches
are still a blur.

What I remember of that afternoon's frenzy
is the August sun,
the dog's unleashed devotion,
and his huge head's grip
on my mind.

A YARD OF TWINE

For Fred Easter, who told me this story

"It takes a yard of twine
to kill a chicken.
You twist one end
around the legs
and hang it high
on a branch or nail
in the barn siding.

"You pluck a few feathers
on the throat
and slit the neck
with one stroke.
Cut as deep as you can.

"Once, from a respectful distance,
I watched a chicken killed.
As it was strung up,
the cows in the pasture
drew near the fence.
The barn and yard went silent.

"The animals watched
the killing too.
They all stared like me
as the chicken was killed
and bled.
They just looked
very quietly
as one of them died."

Would they be silent for one of us?
Would they witness?
Was their silence fear? respect? -
or the resonance with other life
that goes with being
what we call dumb?

MANIFESTO FOR TWO HANDS

For Hilary Sostek

Our friends' daughter demonstrates
her new skill, signing. We watch her fingers
fly through phrases, imprinting on the air
colloquial shapes of how things work, the way they feel.
Delighted, we applaud her "talk."
Accompanying her hands, she speaks the gestures,
and having heard her voice, I know what's missing,
can't imagine how her particular tones,
the quiet melody with self-ironic edge
could be conveyed by hands alone.

Two weeks later, we watch *Children of a Lesser God*
 - and see the genuine, accomplished thing.
Marlee Matlin's signing modulates from polka
to precise ballet of fingers, palms, and wrists.
      Her teacher wants more -
He wants her to speak.
      She remains mute.
He challenges and provokes her.
Forced to having others hear her tongue stumble,
her throat croak, she curses her tormentor out,
fingers spitting obscenities.
In that unvoiced rupture of the silence,
we hear the "Fuck you!" the "I don't give a shit!"

Cursing him who hears what she cannot,
enraged at those who want her to speak words
proud or gentle, she gains a voice.
Exiled from sound, this lovely Caliban,
still making not a sound, makes signs
that shock. In that articulate anger
her gestures' ringing cries resound
and testify for all without a voice.

AT HOME IN THE MIDWEST

They do not see how empty it is,
the natives. Knowing all their neighbors,
not encountering the strange,
they speak a small language of familiar words
and are shy of wild gestures,
even in the hands of children.

The stubble fields and candid sky
companion them like the flattening ground,
the hardening soil on which they write
the concise declarative sentences
of their brief history.

Their dogs bark the space around them,
keeping the new at a distance.
Night arrives on time, no sudden
unknown interiors, no vacancies
they have not discussed
and put by for.

To be at home in the Midwest
is to know it all
from here to horizon,
to inhabit with caution a dream of peace
though the sky fail,
to grapple life from concrete abstractions -
yield per acre,
percentage of moisture.

        And for satisfaction,
to cast or troll for the mystery,
the unnecessary, when the lure,
the shining, gaudy spoon of metal,
brings up from the deeps
something hitherto unpossessed--
wet, silent, vicious, alien,
and finally, demonstrably
there.

SCALDING ANTS

Ants, Grandma! Ants! I cried, amazed at craters
erupted overnight between the flagstones of her walk.
Summer days dry and hot, and suddenly the ants down there
built little fine-grained cones, each with a hole
in the middle leading down through a powdery dirt
I'd never seen elsewhere to a world I tried to imagine.

What did they do besides dig, excavating earth
and piling it all in tiny earthen eggs that the slightest
touch turned to dust? How did they see?
How deep the tunnels down? Were there chambers,
pantries, nurseries? Were they all connected?
How many ants were there? I could never count that many.

Grandma would come to the screen door,
and deliver her lines: "Land's sake,
they're back already." She'd heat a pot of water
to boiling and pick it up in both toweled hands,
carrying it through the screen door with a slam
and saying, *Time to clean this mess up! I hate ants!*

I'd watch her scald and scald,
leveling their eruptions to a thin yellow stain
sluiced into the grass. Drenched and dancing tiny bodies
flooded from the flagstones dark and shining,
corruption washed away, but thousands surviving,
scurrying below, scalded, maimed, angry to return.

We'd do this again and again. She must have thought them dirty,
the result of taint or rot - why else scald and scald?
Why not sweep or hose them off, or even poison them?
They must have meant bad housekeeping,
something sour on her property, so righteous she was,
sloshing boiling water on the darkening stones.

From the safety of the porch's soft-worn wooden floor
I watched the ants' frenzy, drenched again and again
by Grandma ecstatic in her anger. I knew I was
the scouting party calling in their death or torture,
but the power of all that pain, torrents of agony from a height,
all accomplished by my words, delighted me.

FOREIGNER

How mysterious his being is,
complex in its quiet plan
and decorous wants.
His faded jeans look subtly modish,
his cashmere sweater reeks of address,
a costume to be donned and doffed
like a bowler in the City.

I ask. He answers.
We dance the questions -
what he intends, what I require.
I sit here wondering
does he branch left or right?
Is he always subjunctive?
Does he ever rhyme?

We conclude, I guess.
He leaves in a flurry of smile and nod.
A native enters, in native dress.
Without further ado
we get right down to it.

LATE FALL, PLANTING BULBS

For years, come Thanksgiving the ground's like a frozen Snickers Bar;
the pick bounces and the shovel levers up a little clod like a woodchip.
No planting this late. But today, after three inches of melting snow and
two days of rain, sun now shining through a low fog, we plant bulbs in
holes drilled with a metal tube. It has handles and stirrups like a pogo
stick, and when I jump on it to drive it down, it punctures the earth.

We find a patch where, entering th   lrive, we'll receive a floral hello. I
start to clear away the thick pad of leaves gathered around two oaks and
their gooseberry leggings. The rake pulls back layers of leaf and mold.
Next go twigs and broken acorns, uncovering a village of puffballs,
shriveled but whole, that spray dark dust the misty air weighs down.

As I hustle the leaves away I notice a shiny orange dot like a tiny berry
nestled in the soil, then another, and another. For a foot around the
chosen plot, dozens of ladybugs, frost-killed and embalmed in
lacquered coats, speak summer, not this heavy, now darkening autumn.

I rake further, tearing away moss and lichen, down to mammals and their furtive appetites. I see mole tracks, imagine the threat of gophers eating the bulbs, remember mice gnawing the bark of our fruit trees and deer grazing tulips and lilies in the spring. Only heedless reproduction secures this kingdom from its own voracity, and here I stand, a steward in his garden, conceding how little I can do except observe or destroy.

TREEHOUSE

Visiting friends I haven't seen in years.
Long adult conversations, their children bored
to tears, finally our talk must end.
I must see the famous treehouse before I go.
When I look for it my eyes are directed below
to the ground, where I see the beginnings of plywood-
sheathed frame. Looks like a study to me.

For our fourth child I put his treehouse
so high no one weaker could climb it.
He got to the ladder by way of a rope.
It was peril all the way up, nothing but scary space
at the top. No comfort anywhere -
no view without risking a fall.
My son glowed when he ascended
where few could follow. He rose to the dare.
I had just nailed together his hope.

My friends' two children were dearer born,
not plucked like manna by waiting hands.
There were two stillbirths and a fetus deformed -
every time their mother at risk.
After years of danger these children arrived.
Only endless care kept them safe and sound.
Their new treehouse is their father's wish.
It sits solidly on the ground.

MORNING IN THE PARK

She arrives with no face.
Her child, released to dirt from auto plush and glass,
runs toward the sandbox.
She finds a dry bench, brushes it off,
sits down to watch.

She thinks it all too rushed--
"I'm wearing nothing I chose."
Her child - "My child," she thinks - runs towards her,
trips, rights himself, keeps coming.
He has sandy tubes descending from his nose.
His big eyes gleam. His damp hair curls upward.
An invisible and fragrant steam
rises from his head.

He starts to put her face on.
He traces her long nose, fixing it on her face,
thus .!.
He draws a mouth, an even line.

He pats her cheeks
    O   O
on the high cheekbones
and rubbing, brings the blood there.

He makes the mouth lift,
requires a smile and gets it.
Her mouth, no longer straight,
now curves up, the way he wants it.
He smiles back, showing little teeth,
kernels of young corn.
He wants to see her teeth,
to brighten her smile.
Her mouth will open.
She will brighten by and by.

Finally the eyes.
He smoothes the eyebrow--
they want it smooth and gently arched.
He can fill the still pools underneath
with himself.

He plays.
Finally she rises.
Enough park for today.
His arm reaches up to straighten
her arm, aiming it towards him.
He continues putting her together
as they walk away.

LAST CHILD

My fitful young son
slowly enters my dream
and wanders down
the corridors of my affection.

Following on his heels
as he mutters along,
I ask him to repeat his words:
"How's that?"

No reply.

He just looks into each vacant space,
turns, and leaves.
After him I quietly shut each door,
as our procession says goodbye,
room by room,
to this once crowded house.

GRAVEYARD IN VALLEY GROVE: DUSK BEFORE MEMORIAL DAY

No one is there but a single couple
planting family graves with flowers
for Memorial Day. The man hovers
near the gate with wife or sister,
and as I enter makes clear to me
his need to talk.

I turn courteous, stop to chat.
He might be a neighbor I don't yet know.
I ask about the churches - one of stone,
the other clapboard, newer but falling apart.
He is falling apart - with a farmer's tan,
his shirt open on a white beer belly,
a boozer's face, uncertain eyes.
His hand holds a spade like an axe.

"I pumped the organ in that church.
It's a fine pipe organ," he says.
Winter Sundays he climbed the hill.
All the men of his family are buried here,
every one dead in the wars.

He says he's been in Vietnam;
he's damned if he'll be buried here.
"No, not with the other dead men of the family.
Everything all screwed up -
No! Let me be buried far off,
so only God and I know where."

"I won't lock it," he says to me.
"I'll leave the gate open for you,"
I hear as I climb the hill to find my son.
The shameless sunset drenches us,
shadows lengthening in the churchyard,
and the two white buildings bare
beneath the skullcap of the sky.

I tell him what I heard -
a Gothic photograph of needy
solitude and darkness. And when
we leave the yard and close the gate,
I see it has no lock.

URBAN RENEWAL COMES
TO LITTLE CHICAGO

You know the man who installed our plumbing,
the boss's brother-in-law, who sweated two joints wrong
and the boss had to come and solder the joints again
after a pressure check that flooded the basement...
that man with the red hair and freckles,
a red tan, broad shoulders, and mustache...
always talking and smiling a lot.
He smiled and touched you a lot when he talked.
I'd almost forgotten those bad joints.
 - So quick to laugh, always seemed glad to see you?

Well he got a new job driving a fuel truck
from depot to filling stations and had the job
about a month, really proud to be working
full-time again, what with a wife and three daughters.
He'd been laid off so long on account of his brother-in-law
having so little work to keep an extra man,
even a relative, on the payroll.
And he was filling up an underground tank
at a gas station and general store in a tiny place,
really just a wide spot in the road a mile west of US 35,
called "Little Chicago."

He'd gone inside to talk to the owner...
I know Red was talking, and smiling,
and telling jokes - thinking they were jokes -
and he'd left the gasoline tank filling...
because either there wasn't a dead-man switch on the nozzle
or he had figured out a way to outsmart it...
and the tanks just kept filling as he kept on talking,
him not watching the gasoline spilling out on the hot asphalt.
And I can just see him flipping his cigarette butt still smoldering -
that's the way he was, opening the screen door and snapping it out
with a vigorous flick about ten yards - it's a good thing -
like snapping his finger in reverse...
and never looking, intent on the story
and about to come to the point.

Well the place is rebuilt now, bigger, really solid,
like a concrete machinery shed with room in the back for dances -
that's the big draw. I can't remember
if there's any gas pumps...I don't think so.
And I just saw Red downtown in Thomas Market
and he wasn't burned at all...
just sort of lifted up and through the back wall that had blown out,
hardly scratched, real lucky, and he's got another job lined up -
not at a missile base, I hoped -
and he laughed, a little sheepish. But he really seemed
happy to see me again.
And I was really glad to see him
in such good spirits.

* * *

For thirty years I have been teaching and writing. My writing used to consist mostly of letters, memos, lectures, interpretive essays, and an occasional poem, which I didn't take seriously. About ten years ago I changed my attitude when from some rather painless writing, an imaginative piece emerged. The poem was about Russia, and in it I admitted my ignorance of the facts and imagined what that alien territory must be like. It concluded by implicitly comparing the US to the USSR, a relationship that I had not seen before the poem was begun. In my teaching I often confess ignorance and explore the space which that confession opens up, but this was the first time I had tapped those resources in writing a poem.

Another breakthrough came when I remembered an incident from childhood--my grandmother's pouring boiling water on the ants infesting her sidewalk. I remembered, or imagined, calling out to her, "Ants, Nanna, ants!" That sounded like a good start, and I gradually constructed a poem from it that ended up implying how nice young men could become killers in Vietnam. The natural metaphor of scout or forward observer just appeared unsought as I slowly wrote and rewrote.

Having experienced the wonders of catching a lunker, I was hooked. I began to write and especially to revise with the expectation and frequent experience of discovery, which I had previously associated with writing essays but not with poetry.

Now that I am addicted to poetry from both sides of the desk, I have a much better idea of how to read. I know more precisely when and how a poem finds a new relation. In reading I often get ideas for poems from others' work: we learn by imitation, even in middle age. My taste has broadened too. I used to hate narrative poetry. Now since most of my poems tell, or at least imply, an event, I have greater interest in story-telling. In fact, merely lyrical expression seems trivial in comparison to details of a significant narrative. I try, as Hemingway said, to state not the emotion but the sequence of fact and motion that makes the emotion. And I am continually exploring the implications of Emily Dickinson's remark, "Tell all the Truth but tell it slant--/Success in Circuit lies." Since I started writing for others, I have felt her wisdom from the inside and can now help students understand how that principle really works.

Robert Tisdale

MARY MOORE EASTER

CRADLE

I dive,
and heavily weighted,
sink to the dark sea floor
a home where I soon breathe
once a day
and my heart beats
on the hour.

I swell
a giant sea creature
large around myself
all eyes turned inward
not sleeping but still.
Rocks are my companions
submerged mountains
ancient stone, former volcanos.
We bide our time.

I rise first,
outstripping Atlantis
and molten lava,
companions in that watery passage.

Heartbeat increasing by degrees
I peel to filigreed neurocytes,
float,
and finger the water
at shallower plateaus.
My eyes lighten,
lungs surge.

The cradle of the surface
looms above me
a last resting place
before I take to the air.

POEMS ON VISITING THE GIVENS COLLECTION OF BLACK LITERATURE AT THE UNIVERSITY OF MINNESOTA

I

The word sleeps here
locked into safety
preserved by dimness.
Gathered in such a mass
it makes the stillness rumble,
needs to be secured
lest it rip the head off
the unwary researcher.

II

Do not touch too many
of these books.
DuBois' fingers may have
grazed that one.
And the prints of Countee Cullen
are all over those letters.
The words will open
places on your skin
and the ridges of your finger pads
will melt into theirs.
You will see what they saw,
feel their time inside you.
Every picture, every syllable
will caress you with knives
and soon you will answer their thoughts
with a screaming of blood
poured out in the half-lit stacks
of the quiet library.

III *Have you ever wanted to assemble a group of people from different eras for a combustible conversation? This is a list of Black women who have told their truths individually. Look up the ones you can't identify.*

Speak to me, Ann Petry.
Let's talk to Toni
about how it feels.
Maya and Nikki
are only a few shelves away.
Let's get the girls together
and tell the truth.
Call Paule and Ann Schockley over here.
Gwendolyn would add wisdom
to the group.
Who's going to call Ntozake
with her bad mouth?
For truth-telling, she can't be beat.
Naw, I don't mind the movie stars.
Got to have a little glamour
with the grit.
Get Eartha and Lena and Billie
and Katharine D.
That's grit enough
and staying power, too.
Yes, I want Sonia Sanchez here.
She said it once and
she's definitely still talking.
Ask her to call Audrey Lorde
and Audrey can call Barbara Smith
and the whole crowd from the kitchen table.
Tell Michelle (yes, Wallace)
to get herself here in time for the discussion.
All testimonies will be taken.
Margaret Walker can call Alice
and Alice will be sure to get Zora
if it's humanly possible.
Let's look on Mari Evans and be renewed.
And don't forget Phillis
who stood alone and taught an unbelieving world
that we could indeed read and write.
Come on, Angela and Harriet and Sojourner.
And Angelina you have to come out
from under your days for this.

Who's missing?
Oh yeah, all of you all out there,
come on over.
Let's get together
and tell the truth.

IV *For William Melvin Kelley*

Oh, Billy-boy
you were so young
when you made this record
pouring your words out
in your own voice with no caution.

Oh, Billy-boy
four books lined up side by side
all but the last.
It was not stifled in your throat
for that we can be thankful.
It lies in some dirty drawer
splendid in its mystery,
undiscovered,
the plug that could let you speak again.

Oh, Billy-boy
you were so young
when you stopped singing
that new-word song.

V

The fire has burned full circle
around its center,
charred grass, hot and smoking
where I want to go.
From the chill under dark trees
I am drawn toward the light
willing to forsake the pine needle
softness of the earth
to near this sacred fire.
But I cannot cross the
smouldering ashes.
Embers glow
even on the periphery.
I catch their faint warmth
on my bare legs
venturing now closer
now retreating,
eyes glued to the
heart of flame
attending it.

THE BODY SPEAKS

Time passes
and the body speaks when the body's tongue cannot
the hand shakes holding the silent telephone
the knee slips
the foot curls in for protection
the gut sends tremors along an inner fault
plates shift, snag, grind
and the body roars its change,
its resistance, its crumbling cry.
Through its cracks the body speaks a still-burning core
when the body's tongue cannot.

VIOLENCE I

When the fear rises
your eyes glitter
muscles tense
heart sends you
pacing the short hall
between bedroom and kitchen
smoking furiously
shaking off in words
          "Who me? Nah, I'm fine."
the creature that has you
by the neck
claws sunk deep into your flesh.
          (if only you had your knife...)

Habit of attack
habit of defense
brings the past down
on our heads
          grandfather in hiding
          maimed brother
          dog's throat cut
Empty laughter forms
a scant mask when
the past descends
a cleaver into this bed.

A MAN'S HEART

"Oh, he was a quiet man," they told the romantic young girl,
"and he loved women not just to lie with but he would stand up with
them when no one else would. A quiet young man. A woman could
speak in his company. A man could touch his shoulder with his hand
and call out his own heart for review."

Alice Walker in the dedication
to *Good Night, Willie Lee, I'll See You in the Morning*

If a man could call out his own heart for review
       I would call mine out to meet it. There they would sit
       confronting each other, commiserating a bit,
       exchanging phone numbers for future contact.

How a man calls out his own heart for review is not on the
       list of boyhood lessons. So some men learn to wall up
       a heart so tight it can only escape by exploding.
       Others hear it beating and suffer its tremors in the
       dead of night, small earthquakes after the day's
       distractions. Some even take it out to wear on
       their sleeve, but never look it in the eye.

Calling the heart out for review is a different matter. In
       the deep privacy of the soul, (or maybe just in the
       bathroom), some man or other, sometimes sits down face-
       to-face with his heart, asks its ways and wants,
       puzzles over the hard replies, swears at the demands,
       and weeps for every pierced wound. Then he promises
       his heart he'll think it over.

When such a man calls out his heart for review in my
       presence, it will be the start of something big, and
       heart-to-heart, we will begin to speak the language of
       our blood, our bones, the moving muscle
       that centers our lives.

LIVING ON SCRAPS

Hungry for a world
she could not find entire,
she ate its sounds,
consumed its colors.
She treasured pictures of
Spanish tile roofs,
someone else's umber shirt,
spiky orchids glimpsed in
upscale flower markets.
She hoarded inflections,
mannerisms, slight shifts
of weight,
and enshrined them all
like small statuary
in dust-free boxes,
crumbs to stand for
the real thing.

POEM FROM MONDAY'S BLUES

When the fork is taken away
      use the spoon.
When the spoon is taken away
      use your hands.
When the plate is taken away
      eat off the table.
When the food is taken away
      eat grass.
When the grass withers
      eat dirt
      eat clay
      eat ashes
But eat.

LIVING UP TO THE FURNITURE

The door knob sticks when I try to enter
because the furniture has wedged itself tight
in my absence.
"But I only went for groceries"
I explain to my mother's couch
which joins ranks with my sofa
to bar the door.
"...a little food, a little air..."
Her chairs conspire to fill
the dining room.
Rugs from the past
pad my house with pattern
and old conversations.
The pianos whisper
nineteenth-century arpeggios
to each other in the alcove
while heirloom silver clanks on
to the web-cracked platters
about the absence of formal dinner parties.
My grandmother's desk will speak
only of *Oliver Twist* read hearthside
and Sis Sarah's winter visit in 'twenty-five.

This bounty chokes on
barefoot white rooms
decorated with music and one hammock.
What do they care for naked windows
full of light?
They miss their dresser scarves,
the stiff caress of starched doilies.
With the weight of accumulated years,
they gather the past around them
and refuse to let my life in.
And because I am the last,
I have to obey the furniture.

1.

Rugs from the past
still have our footprints on them.
Baby shoe and sneaker
Daddy's football cleats.
Mama's evening dress swept
these stripes into muted shades.
Arabesque, stripe, fringe, nap,
ancestors all,
family.

I unfurl Virginia rugs
on the prairie
and the old life rises
from their plush surface
dented with the weight
of our steps.

2.

The pianos whisper
about my five-year-old lessons
and Mama saying
"Land on the chord with your whole weight!"
until my little finger ached
and overtones twirled and
somersaulted through the living room.

The pianos bickered through
four-hand sight-reading
at a snail's pace
and muted their hammers
patiently when my lesson
was unpracticed for another week.

Today in homage to late gone afternoons
they cross their wires
and hum the blind-fold game,
hum until every vibration
gives way to stillness, to quiet
except in memory.

3.

The absence of formal dinner parties
is a bore to the china.

"Why be blue and white at all,
why bother with Greek maidens and garlands,
raised pattern, fluted edge?
Why *match*
if we are to sit behind leaded glass
while you quick snack
from a paper towel in the kitchen?
We were not made for sandwiches and chips.
We know the groaning table best,
sparkle under candlelight
and yearn for the company of velvet dresses.
Water-pack tuna is not our dish."

They comfort themselves that
Thanksgiving is coming Christmas is coming
though there is no Auntie to bake the pies
and no Brother to make the rolls.
Mama is not there to slice the fruitcake
for the yellow cakeplate
and Daddy cannot mix the eggnog
into the punchbowl.
They do not know the card games are over
and no one will place the pickle just so
beside the Ritz crackers on the salad plate.
And I haven't the heart to tell them.

4.

My grandmother's desk speaks
about the hearthside
about the boxes of books
about the long winter of reading.
It isn't interested in old deeds
and penny insurance policies today.
It only wants to talk of *Oliver Twist*
read in the early dark
while the fire popped
when Mama was a girl.

5.

And because I am the last
I have to obey the furniiture
even though my children do not.
They are not the last. They still
have me standing between them
and eternity
so they do not have to obey the furniture.
They are willing to be kind to it,
to give use and care,
but they are free for lives full of
possible mistakes
brushed away like easy crumbs.

Obedience to the furniture
is a job for the last.
Promoted to keeper of eternity
by hard loss
I must find the dinners for the plates,
wine for the goblets,
velvet guests for the table.
I must keep the pianos entertained
and engage the desk in conversation.
And I must walk cross the rugs
with a certain step.

* * *

As a dancer/choreographer who started writing poetry after years of working in a wordless medium, I am often asked to describe the connection I find between these two art forms.

For me, the impulse to make is the root of all the arts; what one finally produces, and the form one uses, is determined by the nature of the original idea. But once the idea chooses its means, it requires its own separate skills.

My writing springs from a love of words that exists alongside my love of moving, non-verbal images. In my perfomance work I am interested in the juxtaposition of these two elements: dance, essentially wordless; writing, the essential word. I find the tension between their means most interesting when they go about their separate business, linked by such things as simultaneity, atmosphere, rhythm, rather than by pantomimic equivalence. Indeed, it is the kinds of different connections one can find between the two arts that define one's work.

So much for performance. What about the page all by itself ? I find pleasure in the poetry of a plain-spoken language as it often comes from 'ordinary' people. I write to describe, discover, reveal what I have observed, what I have experienced, and what I know. In the end - or in the beginning - that's not so different from the reasons I choreograph.

Mary Moore Easter

SIGRUN LEONHARD

THE FISH

A few years ago, my father started talking. It was around the time of Quax's death, the last of the post war cats. On New Year's Eve, he announced that he was going to stop drinking. Soon after that, he took up jogging. He gave no explanations. When people asked him for the reasons of the abrupt changes in his life style, he said he thought it was a good idea, and discarded any hypothesis as mere speculation. He had made up his mind, and that was that. He also started talking.

At first, the change remained imperceptible, especially in a family where everybody else talked more than their fair share. It started with his staying at the table after dinner, instead of excusing himself with a soccer game or a chore in the basement, where he used to disappear for hours to fix one of the things that so badly needed to be repaired if the house wasn't going to collapse on us. He always thought that that moment was near and lived in the continuous expectation of an architectural doomsday. We could hear him all day, on weekends, producing grinding and howling noises with one of his power saws that set our teeth on edge. He had always made everybody feel guilty whenever they were engrossed in life, without worrying about the state of the house, the security of our jobs, the political future of the country.

So then, out of the clear blue sky of one New Year's Eve, he gave us a different man. We must have looked at him strangely the first times he did not disappear as soon as the necessity to eat and to make arrangements for the following day allowed. We must have paused in our conversation to give him the second required for his exit, for his one line, well, got some things to take care of down there. We gave him the second and maybe waited another few moments for him to rise, with his ceremonial groan, and walk out, with Quax worried and suspicious look on his face. But he didn't take his clue, didn't leave. Well, one of us would go on, distracted. Now that he was going to stay, the conversation had to be rearranged. Certainly, we were not about to talk with the same amount of intimacy with him around. What did he want?

At first, he seemed to just sit around and listen. It took us some time to realize that he was not interested in figuring out what we were up to, and then setting us straight. Once we had taken to talking more freely in his presence, he would sometimes offer comments that went beyond his usual one-liners in which he had summarized and condensed the lessons of his life, like: If you expect too much, you'll end up with nothing. *Quod licet Jovi, non licet bovi.* What's allowed to the Gods is not allowed to the ox.

His new comments came in the form of questions, or asides. Actually, he often seemed to stand aside from himself, not quite there.

You could watch an idea offered to him travelling around in his mind, could see it by the way his eyes wandered off, towards the radio in the other corner of the living room, and beyond it, through the wall. His former reflex of catching it like a sharp object flying through the air, and breaking it for the benefit of all of us, gave way to quiet observation. Maybe he had arrived at a place where those things couldn't hurt him, or when he realized their sharp edges were nothing but the glittering wings of butterflies. He began to enjoy watching the days unfold. I think he discovered pleasure: pleasure without a goal.

If such changes hadn't occurred under the cover of small things, they might have been very disturbing, resulting in loss of job, abandonment of the family. My father could have found himself wandering the streets of Paris, like Rilke, following the sick and the poor on their way into the gutter, ready to die with them out of his new burning wish to embrace every part of life. But he continued to go to work in the morning, though he made more use of his flexible hours, to the job he hated but had wished to excel in to prove you could do it even with the lack of any formal training. Now he was quitting it from the inside, imperceptibly peeling the skin of his soul from the tight fit of the demands made on him. He left his painful attachment to it, and then it left him. From the inside.

Suddenly, his eyes began to look like in his childhood pictures: big, curious, and vaguely frightened. He would tilt his head and look at his plate when someone was talking, as if a direct look might be too intrusive and embarrass the talker. We kept expecting the moment when he would look up and stare us in the face with controlled but raging anger and blurt out how insane our opinions were, how irrational, how we lacked even the basic information to make any such statement at all. But it kept not happening. His gaze would walk out of the window, towards the green of the trees, or stretch out on the neighbor's roof, and yet I knew all the time that he was listening. Something had loosened the cork that the past had plugged into his throat like Snow White's apple, had made him stumble, and live.

This was also the time when I started resenting him less. The government had taken a swing to the right, and Quax, his favorite cat, was dead. He ran into trouble taking part in a demonstration for peace in Bonn, and mentioned it in his bi-yearly letters to members of the family with a sense of satisfaction. Oh, he knew very well where to draw the line, and that he could not afford to let his emotions flow freely, because they would flush out most of his former self with the vigor of a force too long resisted. And he still liked his old structures. When he came home at five, he still enjoyed gathering the magazines and newspapers and putting them on a pile with their sides exactly parallel to the table, hanging up all the coats in the closets. Nothing was supposed to lie around. But even those chores he did with a new lack of enthusiasm, as if the conviction of the usefulness of his order had left him. At times he practiced his grumpy look and paced up and down the two floors with his head between his shoulders and the suspicious look on his face that reminded me so much of Quax, the cat who had been his like none of the others before.

Why do you say that, he would ask, grinning.

I don't know, sometimes you just look like him, I said, you've got this look on your face. Suspicious. Disdainful of human nature. The way you walk across the living room. Sniff the air to see if it's safe. Something like that.

He seemed to think about that, tilting his head, an expression that appeared to be saying, well, maybe... He was a strange cat, he said.

Yes, he sure was. Became stranger as time went by. Why did you always fight with him?

What do you mean, fighting, he said, slightly defensively. We just played. He liked to play.

Oh come on, I said. All cats like to play. But what you did was different. You set him up. You threw him up on the cupboard from where he couldn't get back down, and when he had tried everything and it didn't work, you made him jump on your back. He had to be tough, strong, right? A hero of a cat. You came at him with your fingers outstretched, poking them right in his face, and you made that hissing sound. You tried to scare him. You left him no way out, and then he jumped at your hand. Don't you remember you used to be all scratched and bloody, all of the time?

He liked it, he said. He could have run away, but he didn't.

That is true. Quax would come after him, seeking the tension of the fight. As if bound by a strange mutual contract, they looked for each other, for the pain and the excitement. Come here, Quax, he would yell, and the cat approached slowly, ears folded to his head in anticipation of conflict, but he would come closer, almost creeping, his fat belly touching the ground.

My father grasped him by the loose skin of his neck and hurled him through the air. Sometimes when we saw it, we shrieked with fright. Come on, he would scream, don't be a sissy. Jump! And eventually, the cat answered the call.

I am inventing my father, one of the men whose story is so hard to tell. He certainly did not want to tell it, even after he had started talking. His past, he thought, was one of those that need to be buried, put away, stored somewhere in the attic of one's mind and then forgotten. I assume that he spent a lot of energy keeping it there, forgotten. Maybe that is why the nights did not leave him alone, why they jerked him out of his superficial sleep and sent him wandering through the house at two, at three am.

He tried out various teas and pills. They seemed to work out at first, but after a few hours he would find himself wide awake, staring the night in her face, wondering if he should get up or pretend he could go

63

back to sleep. In the morning, his face was often grey with fatigue, and even after the time he started talking he often fell back into his cold and angry state that made him impenetrable to everybody and everything.

Sometimes, I heard him downstairs when I was up late, working on my school work. After I had enrolled at the University, I used to work at night, into the early morning hours, because they were the only ones when I managed to put the daily turmoil out of my mind and found peace enough to work. He would go into the kitchen to make himself a cup of tea, then sit in the living room with the radio on, although, as he told me some time later, he had to be very careful with music; it had the power to undo him completely, to throw him into a state of unthinkable sadness. Why? He shrugged his shoulders. He did not want to tell, maybe he did not know.

I am inventing my father. It is hard work, because what there is to tell is so slender, and what is worth telling I cannot prove. It grows out of those nightly hours when I heard him pacing around the house, out of a few snippets of conversation so carefully measured that I felt one question too many and he would go back into the facade of his angry stone face. No, he would say, enraged, he had not been afraid during the air raids. You've got to understand, he said, everybody was going through this. Berlin, what do you expect?

But your house was bombed three times, wasn't it? And then, didn't you get stuck in the rubble once, for an entire day or so?

He nodded, briefly, as if to cut it off. Yes. The house collapsed on us. But I was 12, 13 at the time, and it all seemed like a big adventure. When we still had school, we would walk over dead bodies in the morning to get to class. Lots of dead bodies.

But you must have been scared, I said. Terrified.

He looked impatient now. Enough of this. Naw, he said, it was a big game for us. We were kids. We collected the bomb shells in the morning, we tried to construct bombs. Adventure, you know. At that age, everything is adventure. We thought nothing of it, not of the dead bodies and not of the people who had been hit by the phosphor bombs and were running through the streets burning, trying to get to the canals. Then they would jump into the water and dive, but you see, when they came out, they would just go on burning. That's phosphor for you. They just kept on burning. Torches.

There must have been a time when he still went fishing, but not for the catch any more. He couldn't sleep anyway. He would get up an hour before dawn, since right around dawn is the best time. We were all sleeping in our different bedrooms, my mother stirring in her bed as he left, clothes in his hands. The night was breathing quietly, and he did not want to wake anybody up.

He must have felt like I did during my late study hours. I had made myself a pot of herb tea and carried it up to my room. I had closed the

64

door. They were all sleeping downstairs, all but him, maybe, calmed down for the next eight hours or so. I liked the idea that they and their difficult love were asleep now, tugged into the warmth of their beds, unable to harm themselves or each other. The silence that held them seemed almost holy to me, merciful in the forgetfulness it placed on their foreheads like a cool hand. I could feel the tension leaving the house, sometimes so tangibly that I would sit on the stairs to the second floor, looking out through the window, letting myself feel the relief of our sleep-induced togetherness. On those nights, I wanted to become the staircase, or the glass window. I thought those incarnations would be easier to bear, and yet preserve the sense of community that I didn't want to give up.

I often listened to the radio on those late nights, while I was reading or writing a paper. In the summer, the window was wide open, and let in the breezy talk of the trees, or the thunderstorm, or the comforting face of the moon. Today I wonder if it didn't start then, my gliding off the window sill and travelling into space.

My father must have had similar feelings when he got up, just two or three hours after my solitary late night ecstasy had been crushed by fatigue. I rarely heard the garage door open. He was very quiet. He took a piece of bread along, and a thermos of black tea. Sometimes, he participated in contests, and once he came home with a basket full of fancy foods, the first prize, proud and happy. During the last years, he had stopped going to the contests. I think he went to be near the lake at the hour when it woke up with life, to see the sky turn a lighter shade of dark, and then the first cool strip of muted silver on the horizon, above the hills. The first morning light unveiled to him, and to him alone, the dewy branches of the willows on the edge of the small lake, and dipped them into a new color tone every few minutes. He stood in his thigh high green rubber boots, cold and tired, and wished for nothing. Least of all, I presume, for a fish.

I think of him the last time he went out, lost in his thoughts or lost in the soft shimmer of the lake, its smell at dawn, lost in the early chirping of the birds. The first cars made noises along the highway in the distance. The sun was barely above the horizon, a tumbling ball of orange fire dipping the lake and the hills around it in a reddish light. There were some water lilies he hadn't seen before, just on the verge of opening, as if looking through their fingers like children who don't want to be seen. The grass was so fine that he thought he didn't want to leave tracks with his heavy boots.

Suddenly, he felt a jerk in his hand, reminding him why he was there. He pulled in the line mechanically, slowly, an expert. It was difficult. He knew immediately that this was a big one. The carp didn't want to come out and still struggled when he held it in his hands and pulled the hook out of its mouth. Fish can't close their eyes, not even when you hit them against a stone, or take out your knife to cut their throats. My father looked at the wriggling carp for a second as he felt for the knife in his pocket. Maybe the carp looked at him, pleadingly, or with hatred, or just with the blank stare of panic. Was it surprised to find itself back in the water with a sudden splash? Or did it come away from the encounter remembering it only as a faint vision of one strange Sunday morning?

My father wiped his hands on his pants and went over to the can with the worms to put another one on the hook. There was always an unpleasant sensation of resistance when you put a worm on the hook, as if you jammed a knife into skin that first resisted the pressure but then gave in with a small, dull sound. He stared at the entangled life of the worms in his can. He took one out, looked at its transparent roundness, the flesh colored rings it seemed to be made of. Such stupid things, worms. When you cut them in half, both parts will wriggle on through their pedestrian lives. Such determination to preserve so little. He emptied the can into the wet grass, packed up his fishing equipment, and drove home.

He never went fishing again. Every once in a while, someone will ask him why, and comment on what a waste it is to have all that beautiful equipment hanging in the garage. The mice kept eating my sandwich, he will say. And then, I felt sorry for the fish. People laugh, and he smiles. He wants it to be a joke. He will not admit that he almost cried, that morning, on the carp's panting face, paralyzed by its lack of comprehension.

He still does not like to tell his story, not the right way. I have to do that, in the first morning hours when everybody is asleep, and he has not woken up yet to his hours of insomnia. I walk towards him in his sleep and say: tell me about the carp, how it looked at you. How you threw it back, and why. Tell me why you really did it. And only then, when the night is thick with darkness and the despair of the past, when I stay awake from tea and memory and the pressure of all his unspoken words, only then a dark room in my mind opens behind the headache and the tears, and he tells me.

tough cookie

someone asked me, the other day,
about the future: ten years from now.
where do you want to be, he said,
with the kind of smile that's supposed
to evoke dim eyed answers.
where would you like to be in your life, dearie?

he didn't mean places, he meant
would that kid be still living with me,
or with his father. would I have a job
that would make me a respectable companion,
challenging, but not a slap in the face
of a man in need of worship. he meant
how would I juggle it, work and all.
something like that.

it took me a while to ponder
the possibilities. the lights were out,
the movie had already started, and he
had forgotten about his question
when I said: you want to know?
you really do?
I want to be a tough cookie,
that's what. I want to walk
through the streets at night unafraid
with a swiss army knife in my purse.
I want to enjoy my life,
what's left of it, without considering
if you like my tough cookie looks
and politics. I'll know exactly
what's going on around me
and won't mince my words
when they hand me the microphone.
that won't get me a good job
or an adoring husband,
won't make me a prominent figure
in church activities,
but I know it will feel
very refreshing.

the cynic's journal

1. Joanne

she never wanted to live
on the outskirts of society.
she stayed with her husband and two sons
with behavioral problems but
all the time I knew Joanne
her lovers were women.
she liked to kiss them
between doors, in attics,
enjoyed the thrill with the musty smell
of secret places.
paul knew but ignored
the details: women,
he used to say at cocktail parties
(champagne and shrimp salad
in avocados)
are naturally close, enviably
intimate, and men, he used to say
could learn from them.
in the morning he went
to the bank where family money
worked for both of them.
he wasn't going to make himself depressed
by trying to understand
what was happening to them.
that's why she stayed: he was
easy to despise.

II. Jonathan

watch his face twitch: life
makes him nervous. he would like
to quit it more often than not,
but doesn't have too much time
to consider it. being famous, well,
within the profession,
brings along too many obligations,
which is one of the reasons he feels
like life is nothing but a rat race,
which in turn is so sick, so
sickening, he thinks, that he can only
forget it by working more.

III. Andrew

not too much catches his interest.
almost nothing will hold it.

during most of the conference lectures
he thinks about sex, and who
might be a likely candidate. most women
look worn out by academia, like
dried up plums, grown
under artificial light.

not that the men look any better.
but he isn't interested in them.

IV. Michael

the way you know him, he sits
in a room and practices empathy.
only rarely do his thoughts
wander in a direction that baffles
the client, revealing a piece
of himself, not enough
for a picture.
an expert on suffering,
he will tell you how much,
just how much life has in store.
(where he gets his information
cannot be ascertained.)

V. Nicholas

his is the kind of gentleness never
repaid: women confide in him
as a friend, then
go on dates with the other guy
who makes more tearful conferences
necessary. men say he is nice
and treat him with a certain
lack of respect, because he is,
after all, not a real fighter, not
a big success, not, when you
come right down to it, someone
you would envy.

questions for the gods

where were you when everything got off on a wrong start
so that no matter where we are today we can't do it right
yes, right according to our own concepts, but what else
is there, no guidance from above, not from you
and as for freedom, if you were so intent
on giving us this great gift, then why
not make us so that we can choose
freedom instead of being locked
in our characters - if not jails
and poverty - why, if you
made us, not make us able
to choose the better thing,
and why let it look
like giving in is your
bitter victory and
our defeat?

story hunter

                    you
        look for a smart little plot
        in everyone's gestures
        walk the streets in search of
        ideas everything is material to you
        someone falling off the bus
        the grain of salt that makes
        a new thought crystallize
        your deep gaze is
        the concentration
        of butterfly collectors
        you gourmet of life-lines
        for whom the breakdown
        of someone's composed self is
        caviar

learning how to say goodbye

take the bridges, for instance;
their assertion of relative eternity
as they frame the trembling sunsets with black arches.

the way they lift from the waters
patterns of changing visions,
themselves unchanging,

and watch the Mississippi take along
the memory of parks and power plants and houses
and different kinds of banks,

the beds of shrubbery, the steep
majestic cliffs - forever, or at least
for one short span of life.

the sandstone will outlast countless goodbyes -
and yet I feel: the match
that lit its beauty was your presence,

your hand, so small by contrast,
so immense by meaning, the frame
that brought the city's atmosphere to life.

like the river, I say,
back on the bridge,
moving across its shadow on the waters,

the river with its many films
of images, and all must go, and all are kept
in some deep layer of its endless body -

I will be always here and always leaving.

* * *

It always puzzles me when people ask me why I write. Could it be that they really don't know ? Is it a trick question ? Are they testing me ?

I write because it is a way of continuing to talk when everyone is busy, or exhausted, or otherwise occupied: your parents have finally heard enough about it, and it isn't their fault, anyway; your best friend has a hair appointment followed by choir practice; your lover calls from New Orleans with a head-cold and a bad temper; your colleagues want to discuss the new sub-committee of the curriculum committee, and your students would appreciate some helpful hints as to whether and , if so, in what form Christa Wolf's latest incomprehensible novel will be on the next test. And you are the one who has to write the exam.

Yet the thing at the back of your head, the gun against the inside of your skull says: write this, or I'll kill you - that voice does not take too well to explanations about time-constraints, syllabi and the like. Should you decide to ignore the demands of the alien inside your head, there will be no blood. But be assured that your life will be miserable. You will be creeping, spiritually speaking, on all fours, your knees scraping the ground while you are supposedly enjoying yourself at a pesto dinner. Whether you are at your committee meeting, or sweeping the garage, or even listening to Vivaldi, you will be paying for your sin, the only one, of not saying, not writing what needs to be said and written. Life needs many drafts. Start early.

Sigi Leonhard

WAYNE CARVER

PLAIN CITY
Portrait of a Mormon Village

We have read of the noble deeds of the great and mighty among all nations. We have admired acts of service and sacrifice in many different ways. But when we learn from the facts of that memorable battle for [irrigation] water during the summer of 1859 by this band of Plain City pioneers, whenever we stand on Plain City soil, we will almost feel like one of old: "Remove thy shoes from thy feet, for the ground whereon thou stand is holy ground."

P. M. Folkman, unpublished manuscript

Plain City, Utah, is my home town. The village of this portrait is gone. It lives only in the memory of those of us who were there before 1960. The farms and town lots have been sold off and built on. What was once a sleepy small town of about 800 people is now an ugly suburb of 4000 in an area of aero-space and other military-industrial enterprises. Some of the old buildings and homes exist, used and unused. Some of the people I knew when I was a boy still live there.

I still go back when I can. I am trying to research, remember, and record what the old town was like, somewhat the way Ronald Blythe does in *Akenfield: Portrait of an English Village*. I call my going back "research." What I really do is more selfish than "research." I go to hear those old timers talk. It is good to hear people still using a language as if they owned it, a language that is created out of their memories, experiences, prejudices, angers, loves, nostalgias.

I said to Ellis Lund. "A lot of people in the county think the people in Plain City are stuck up. Think they're better than anybody else."
"That's a crock," he said. "Who said that?"
"I don't know. Somebody from Hooper."
"Oh, well. Hell! *Hooper ?*"

Joe McGrue wrote in a book that in 1912 John Carver, 90, lay dying in Plain City and refused to pass away until he talked with his son Lewis. Lewis came and told his father once again of the trip he had made to heaven when he was on his mission. Everything on the other side was ready for him. They were waiting. The Patriarch died peacefully.
"That's an odd story," I told my Dad's cousin, Lee. I showed him the book. Lee did two missions for the Church He read the story.
"Nothing odd about it," he said. "The odd thing is you've been in school all your life and still don't know horseshit when you read it."

I asked a lady in the town if she knew what Kolob was. She said she had no idea.
"I think it's in the *Book of Mormon*," I said.

"Probably is," she said. "Or I might of heard of it. I don't know anything about my religion. I just live it. I know what I'm supposed to do and I do it."

"That's fine," I said. She looked at me hard.

"There's some others might try it," she said.

I could go on I probably will, another time, another place.

Now listen to three guys I grew up with tell about World War II, a war that didn't really bother Plain City until the draft started to take our ball team. These monologues are made out of hours of recorded conversations. The transcribed tapes often run to fifty or sixty pages. I've tried to extract threads, then spin the threads into yarns.

WAR IN THREE VOICES

Norman E. Carver
b. 1919

Paul Knight and I grew up together in Plain City, rode horses, played ball, did everything. Went to school. And in February of 1941, with the draft staring us in the face, we volunteered for our year of service. There wasn't much work and no money for college. We figured we would get the service out of the way. Paul got out five years later, over three of them in the Pacific fighting. By the end of the war, I was in the Air Force. I stayed in until '46. I loved flying.

When we went in, everything was World War I. Wrap-around leggings. High collared tunics. Springfield rifles. At Fort Lewis we saw one of the first jeeps ever to make it into a unit. So we were told. We had those little flat steel hats. I never did have an M-1, not personally. That's a long story.

At Fort Lewis, Paul was assigned to a machine gun unit, a light Browning machine gun was his weapon. I did basic with the Springfield. After that, I was passed over for PFC, if you can imagine. Everybody that went in got their PFC stripes but me. I was pretty upset. It meant six dollars a month. Out on the rifle range, I did pretty well with the Springfield. Then I was assigned to the Browning Automatic Rifle squad. And I set a new regimental record with the BAR. The next day I'm called into the Captain's office - Captain Lonigan, the CO - and he said, "W^e have an opening for a corporal in that BAR squad and we're transfer ing a guy out. We want you to be corporal." And I said, "I'm not even a PFC yet." He said, "What happened?" And I said, "I don't know." He said, "We'll cut orders and make you a corporal."

So two days passed, and I got called back, and the Captain says, "The sergeant of that BAR outfit has been moved, and we're going to make you sergeant instead of corporal." I said, "That's fine. I can get along with that all right." So I was given the buck sergeant stripes. Never was a PFC or a corporal. I started to instruct on the BAR - field stripping, sight pictures, and all of that. People think the BAR is a complicated piece. It isn't. Its complication is its weight - seventeen pounds. Then all the ammo you had to carry for it. It was clip fed, up to twenty round clips. It fires 650 rounds a minute, but you can't feed in the clips that fast, of course.

After maneuvers in the California desert, the Japanese hit Pearl Harbor. Nobody I knew knew where Pearl Harbor was.

We were loaded on trucks at Fort Lewis and moved to the Boeing plant in Seattle to guard the planes. That's the first time in my life I am up close to a big airplane. So I disperse my two squads around this airport and guard the B-17's and the A-20's that were being shipped to England. They all had British markings on them. So here you are out there standing guard and two young kids with parachutes over their shoulders come and climb into that big old bird and fly it out of there. They just looked like ordinary people to me. I - you know - I thought aviators were something else, that you just read about them, I guess. I decided that that was for me, right then and there.

*

Our applications for transfer to flight school in the Air Force came back rejected. Captain Holmes said, "They can't do that to you." "They've done it," I said. "Send them in again," he said. We did and they came back. "Transfer between units not authorized at this time." We were pretty blue, but, you know. You take it in stride.

By this time it's about January 15th, 1942, and we shipped to Fort Dix with the regiment, 162nd Infantry, 41st Division.

At Dix I got hold of Murray and Moore, the guys that had applied for flight training with me, and I says, "We're going to end up in Australia. How are we going to get back here for flight training from Australia?" Moore says, "Ah, they'll have means of doing it." I says, "We'll never make it." Old Murray says, "Hey, I know a guy down at headquarters. Let's talk to him. He's a minister. He's got a lot of pull."

So we get down there and the minister's a master sergeant with a major's gold leaf on his collar. Out of the reserves. He must have been somebody's invention. He says, "Your cause is just, but there's nothing I can do for you." Then he thinks for a few minutes. "I'll write a telegram and send it to the right people if you'll sign it, but I won't put my name on it." What have we got to lose? So he writes the telegram and gives it to us to sign and we see that it's to "Chief of Staff for Air, H.H. Arnold." We didn't see anything wrong with going right to the top. So we signed it. We sent off that telegram that night and about one o'clock in the morning an orderly woke me and says, "Pack your stuff. You've been transferred." So I get my gear together in the dark, you know, and meet Murray and Moore downstairs. So I says to them, "Now what do we do? They won't even let us sleep in the barracks. We've been transferred with a thirty-day delay enroute to Maxwell Field." Old Murray says, "I've got another friend." By this time it's mid morning. We go with Murray and find this young lieutenant in some headquarters. He's got a brand new 1941 Plymouth and he's going to Australia and he's fit to be tied. He wants that car delivered to Portland, Oregon, and that's where Murray lived. Murray says, "If you treat us right, we'll take your car to Portland." So we loaded our gear in this brand new '41 Plymouth and headed out across the bridge out of New Jersey, cross country, down the Pennsylvania Turnpike. Sixty-one hours later, Murray's in Portland, and I'm in Plain City. I never saw Paul again until, oh, it must have been 1945 or 6 when we were both in Plain City, me on leave. He had one rough war.

*

When we got back to Agra, Taj Mahal country, we couldn't get out. No planes. We went to Operations and said give us a plane and we'll fly it. This guy says they've got a C-46 loaded and ready to go but nobody around is qualified in C-46's. I whipped out my card. Hadn't flown one in six months, when I took one to London. So we got out and back to base, but we almost took the spires off the Taj Mahal. The gear handle was all bent up and we had a hard time getting lift.. But it worked out all right . . .

Flying that hump was something. We flew as much as a hundred to a hundred and twenty hours a month all the time we were there. Flew from Jorhat in the upper Assam Valley to all over the central part of China.

We never flew with the same crew. You'd fly with some guys and never see them again. I drew this flight with Jack Enlowe. Jack had been out there a long time, lot of trips. As we landed at Luliang, just on the stroke of midnight, the right tire on the B-24 blew out when it touched down. The plane swerved about forty-five degrees to the runway and went off through the boondocks, wiped out all four engines, all four props broke off, all three landing gears folded, and the plane started to come to pieces and caught fire. We were loaded with hundred octane fuel. That's all the cargo we had. The crew chief got the hatch open and he and the radio operator went out on top of the plane while it was still moving. I got the side window open, as soon as the plane stopped, and I went out that window and met the radio man and crew chief in front, right in front of the plane. We looked for Jack, and he had his head and shoulders out of the hatch, but couldn't get his body out. We ran back to him. Somehow he lurched out, and we grabbed him and dragged him and his left leg from the knee down was just wobbling loose. We knew it was broken clean off. We dragged him, oh, maybe thirty or forty yards, into behind a little bank of dirt that was thrown up there. Then the plane blew, started to blow. It didn't blow in one big blow. But it went BOOF, BOOF, BOOF - and it completely consumed that plane in a matter of ten or fifteen minutes.

Whew! That was close and hot. Then we saw some headlights coming from Operations. I had a flashlight in my jacket and I stood up and waved it back and forth. There was four people in that jeep and they missed us by about a foot, went right past us. They had their eyes on the fire. They were coming to pull us out of the plane. Well, things calmed down and we loaded Enlowe on the back of that jeep and cradled his broken leg, got him in, got the doctor out of bed, cut Jack's pants off. It was just like a heap of hamburger, that whole knee. They stabilized him and shipped him out. The next time I saw Jack was in our home in Kennewick, Washington - in about 1983 or so. But that's a whole other story. He died not long after that.

But that crash landing in China. Man. I went back out there the next morning and scrounged around in the ashes and there was a pool of aluminum, just like a bathtub, about that thick. That airplane melted down and just all flowed into a low place and set up. But, you know, when we crashed, I went out the side window with such enthusiasm that I caught my coveralls on my military 45 and ripped it out - just like that. The safety officer investigating the accident said, "Now you went out the side window of a B-24?" I says, "I did." He says, "You'll have to show me how you did that. Nobody can get out the side window of a B-24." And I says, "Well, I did." Well, we went out and we couldn't find a B-24 that I could get my head out of the side window of, let alone my body. But this one must have been different, cause I sure went out of it. Or maybe I took the window with me.

They put me on another B-24 that night, back to the base in Jorhat, as a passenger. I was ok until the landing. But as we began to touch down, I sure hoped the tire didn't blow. It didn't.

* * *

Harold Ross
b.1923

My name is John Harold Ross I was born in Rupert, Idaho, Novemeber 7th, 1923. After two years my mother passed away giving childbirth, and so my father gave us to my mother's family down in Plain City. We were Milo and Paul and my sister, June. In Plain City we lived out on the north end of town - well, you know that, Wayne - by the creamery. Milo was raised by Ed Sharp and his family. Paul by Fred and Vic Hunt. Howard Hunt's folks, you know. He was killed in the war, in Italy or some damned place. June went to Ogden and was raised by Mark Streeter and his wife, who was mother's sister. All this was arranged by Oz Richardson and I never saw my real father again. Can't remember ever seeing him.

I was raised by Del and Violet Sharp, who I call Mother and Dad. Del's father had left the Church. But after X amount of years, I was baptized and did all the Church things. But you know that. We did them together.

There have been so many people in this Plain City ward that set their efforts and goals to help myself and my brothers take a part in this community and in the Church and in our everyday living. Albert Sharp, who I call my brother. Your dad, Elmer Carver. The Hipwells and Englands. Walt Christianson. All those fine, fine people. They never stopped walking beside me and kept me as good as I have been, which hasn't been very good, according to a lot of people. I was always a hand-me-down. I was the blacksheep of the whole tribe. But those people acted like I wasn't . That's saved me.

I enlisted in the army in April, 1942. At this time it was double time and hut hut to overseas. I spent six weeks at Camp Beal in California, then right to Australia. My outfit was the 540th Armored Infantry Battalion, but in the jungles you cannot use armor. So the 540th was dissolved, and I was assigned to the 32nd Division, which was a Michigan-Wisconsin National Guard outfit, and I went into combat with them.

We walked the Owen Stanley Mountains which took forty days and we encountered Japanese forces at all times. We hit the town of Buna and we received the name of the Buna Butchers when we overrun a headquarters and a hospital and I guess we - uh - done tremendous damage. That was in December of '42. After that we went all the way up the coast. I think I was on every island in the Pacific, either landing with the whole outfit or with special units. I was a gung-ho young man. Once we went in by PT boats and secured an island and when we came down from the hills, I ran into Paul Knight, a McFarland kid from West Weber, Lym Skeen from Plain City - he pitched some after the war. Big slow roundhouse out - you know - and a lot of Weber County kids. We could have started a ball league right there on the beach.

*

I came home in '46. When I got off the train in Ogden, Harold Hunt and Ellis Lund and somebody else came in from Plain City and got me. My folks didn't have a phone. I called the beer hall and asked if somebody could come and get me. Then later in that year I married. Her dad was Butch Hancock in West Weber. You know him. Her uncle lived in Plain City, down on the sandhill by Alvy Weatherston.

I went to work for Swifts, selling meat, for $18.50 a week, no commission. Then I had a son. I re-enlisted back into the service and went to Fort Ord in California. I was a tech sergeant then. Then a master sergeant. Then they activated the Second Division which was the big Indian Head Division in Fort Lewis, Washington, and I stayed there and trained it, then went to Hawaii. Then we came back from Hawaii to Fort Lewis. Then we turned around and shipped to Korea where we were getting our hindquarters whipped royally. I took over a company. By that time I had a commission.

So we went in in the fall of '50 and like I said I was commissioned a second lieutenant, and took over a company and I got wounded and my greatest desire was to get home for Christmas and Christmas day I got home. They evacuated me to Travis Air Force Base in California. I had my choice of what hospital I'd go to, and I said I'll go to Denver to Fitzsimmons. They still hadn't treated the wound very much. I don't think any, but they must have some. But I could feel it bleeding. So I was going to Fitzsimmons at Denver. It was just a day or two before Christmas. I said I sure would like to go home for Christmas, and they says, "If you can find a way home, you can go." So I went to the supply room and saw some people getting into parachutes and I says, "Where you going with the parachutes?" And they says "We're getting a hop out of here." And I says "Anybody going to Hill Air Force Base ?" "And some major was there and he says "I am." And I says, "Can I go with you?" And he says, "You can if you can get a parachute." Well, I couldn't find no parachute but I found the bag, you know, that looked like a parachute if you didn't look too close. So I just throwed it across my arm and we came to Ogden. Hell! I was hobbling on crutches because I'd got this bullet wound in my back which lodged near my spine. It was still bleeding. I could feel it. But I wanted to get home, so I didn't say anything. It never hurt much. So

81

there I was in Ogden, ten miles from home in West Weber. I lived in West Weber at that time. I called but didn't get anybody at home and so, I think it was that gentleman, the major that flew me to Hill Air Base, he gave me a ride out to West Weber. I left there right after Christmas and took my wife and son to Denver and went to Fitzsimmons and I was there, I think, two or three months. They done an operation on me and they lined this bullet in my back with silicon and I never had no problem. Still got the bullet in there. You can feel it if you want to....

*

Two or three months later, I left Fitzsimmons on a Friday from the airport in Denver and went to Travis. We refueled at Travis and then we flew to Hawaii and fueled and right on overseas over the International Date Line. I got out of the airplane in Korea about 12 miles from my unit. We had radioed ahead, and I had a jeep there to pick me up. I got into the jeep and went to my company. I got my equipment. We got about two miles up the road going toward the lines when I got hit. Two slugs in my leg from a hand grenade. They got me back out of the fire, took me to that same landing strip, and I got on approximately the same airplane, only it was a different airplane, that was flying back to Hill Air Force Base. I flew back, got off the plane at Hill, got on another one and flew to Fitzsimmons General Hospital and was back in the same hospital and it was Monday morning and I hadn't been gone but since Friday.

After recuperating, my orders were cut again and I accepted the privilege of going as cadre to the Infantry School at Fort Benning, Georgia. When I got down there, I was two weeks behind in a survival school that my name was on to go through. I was a survivor of two wars and two bad wounds so I had to go to school in the woods of Georgia to learn how to survive.

Well, it came time to go on this wilderness survival deal for two weeks. I had never jumped. Everybody else had, from the tower and things like that. I didn't know anything about jumping, except in and out of fox holes. I wasn't drinking then. But I thought it might be a good time to start. I was over at the officers' club there one night and ran into the pilot that flew the plane we were to jump out of. So I made a point of getting right acquainted with him. He explained to me, "You be the last one off that plane." And I said, "Well, I'll assure you of that." "When you're out," he said, "we'll fly back over you and you try to follow the plane." I said, "OK." I wasn't scared then, not until the next day. Next day, up there, everybody else is gone, and they finally push me out. I'm falling and I looked around for that plane. Nowhere. So I got ready to hit the ground - I'd been reading their brochures, you know, to jump a little bit and to raise your feet and to relax a little bit, and all those great things. Next thing I knew something hit me all over and dust was flying all over my face and this parachute flowing round and around me and I was like a big bull in the china closet. Then I hear this plane and it came in low and tipped his wings and I waved at him. So I thought I'd follow his directions because he told me to go that way.

I walked all day, all day long. I didn't come to no roads, no nothing. I cursed that pilot. So I laid down. When I woke up I could hear honks, you know, car and truck honks. I went over and about three or four hundred yards away was the highway. So I walked along it and came to a really fine motel. I checked in, called my wife in West Weber. She came and stayed with me. Two weeks later she came back home. I rubbed some dirt in my beard, took a taxi out to the Infantry School, and taught survival training to green officers. I had the privilege of having John Eisenhower go through one of my classes.

Seems like a long time ago. Yeah, I've stayed with the Church - off and on. I'm not as active as I should be. But I go and believe and I have my children go and they are baptized. I'm double pensioned now from the Army and from Hill Field. I only worked at Hill about 120 days, when I was still in the Army, but I get a full pension. The records got screwed up. I'll tell you how that came about, but it's a long story....

* * *

Paul Knight
b. 1919

...but you can't forget the people in this town back then, when we were kids. It was just a good town to live in. Just Plain City. A dinky little country town. If you got sick, everybody pitched in, helped you get the work done. Remember when the whole town turned out and got your Dad's onions in, took a couple days, when Norm's little black pony stumbled and threw your dad and broke his hip? You bet. And every morning we herded the cows through town to the West Pasture. Then at night somebody would turn them out and they'd drift toward home. They'd get up on the ball diamond and we'd go up there and cut out our herd and take them home and milk them. Then after milking we'd go back up to the square and practice ball until dark, trying to stay out of the cow shit. Then that sandburr patch along the short-stop spot! Nobody had any money. Oh, there were problems.

You know the two proudest days of my life? Happened right here and with my folks. One was the first day I went to school, first grade. Mother bought me a new pair of striped overalls - Scrowcroft Never Rips. Remember them? And I had short socks on. Remember when we was dressing up for Sunday school we'd have those long socks that come up over your knees, like knee pads. Merrill Jenkins wore them until he was eighteen, I know for a fact. But there I was six and had a new pair of striped overalls and short socks. I went out on the front steps. Dad was down by the barn hitching up the team to go to the farm at West Warren. I had to slip down there and tell him. I think he knew, though. He never said nothing when I showed him, but he was grinning. He was as proud as I was, I think.

The other time was a little later. Dad let me drive the team from our place in Plain City to West Warren. Dad's team was a proud team that was kind of noted for running away. They'd run away with the wagon from time to time. And he let me drive them, alone. Boy, I strutted all day after that.

Yes, we was just a close town that everybody was proud to be a part of. We all went to Church, all us young ones. But baseball was the real religion. This town went crazy over baseball. I saw a miracle once. Gene Maw - old Gene - was with us and we had ridden our bikes and horses to West Weber for a ball game. And Gene was sitting out in the field, right field. He's just got tired and was kind of dozing off. And one of them big Greenwell bucks from West Weber - used to catch - got up to bat and slammed one like a rifle shot out toward Gene. Everybody yelled and Gene just thought they were yelling at him for sitting down and he stuck up his glove hand to wave to them and that damned ball hit right into that mittt and stuck. Did we laugh! I'll never forget that. And you know, that happened a long time ago and I still see the look on old Gene's face when that ball hit. And the rabbit hunts we had. And the dances. Every Saturday night, it seemed like. And the Fourth of July up on the square. Shit, man!

Things have changed in this town. Hell, you don't know anybody any more. You couldn't drive a cow through town now. You'd cause a panic and get arrested by some stranger in a car marked "Plain City Police."

And then I guess the army would be about the next deal, when things was looking like war and they started the draft up. Norm came over one day. I don't know, we was sitting there talking. You had to go in for a year. I said, "Let's go into town and join up and get it over with." So Norm and I went in and enlisted.

We got down to Fort Douglas and bumped into some guys we knew who had been drafted. Wayne Kennedy was one, I remember. Jack Charlton from West Weber. Claude Jardine from Taylor. Joe Martin from up here in Farr West. We all went to Fort Lewis together. Some of us stayed together. Old Joe got killed. Down there at Douglas they interviewed us and volunteers were supposed to get your pick of the branch of service you wanted to be in. I don't know what Norm told them. I told them cavalry. That was always the way of life I liked, around horses. So they sent me to the infantry. So much for the interview.

Well, we trained at Fort Lewis from February , 1941, to December, with a couple months down there in the California desert with rattlesnakes and scorpions. Them scorpions, they were thick.

We was in the 41st Division. I was in the 163rd Regiment. Norm the 162nd. After Pearl Harbor, Norm's outfit was sent to Fort Dix and went through the Panama Canal to Australia. They was on the water some 40 odd days. Norm had gone to the Air Force by then. The 163rd went to San Francisco, got on the Queen Elizabeth, and we all hit Australia the same time. God I was sick. First time I had ever seen the ocean.

There was one good time in that California desert in them maneuvers. We had a sergeant - we called him "Bear Meat" - and we'd caught a big rattler. Old Bear Meat had to have his nose in everything and one of us held the snake's mouth open and somebody else took a knife and pushed down on one of its fangs. Some of that stuff squirted out and hit old Bear Meat right in the eye. It must have hurt a lot and we told him he was going to go blind. But he didn't. Anybody but Bear Meat would have. We had a laugh over old Bear Meat.

But back to the Pacific. Our first combat was New Guinea. We landed at Port Moresby and I end up in the hospital with a temperature of 105. Malaria. I was out of it for a month.

I got back to my outfit and we made a landing way up the beach in New Guinea. We didn't hit anything much. We made another landing farther up and hit nothing to speak of there. That's where Harold Ross came in. Walked into my tent and I was sitting on my cot sharpening a new issue - those trench knives that you could use as bayonets, too - and Harold came up behind me, put his hand on my head and started to push down. Hell, I swung up and around with that knife and cut him across the back of one his hands. Old Harold. "I come all the way from Plain City to see you," he said, "and you try to kill me." He wasn't hurt. We laughed about that.

Some of the landings we made were against pretty heavily defended places. Old Harold's 32nd Division took some tough places and a lot of losses. But we got in in good shape. Old General MacArthur - thought he was one of the best generals the U.S. Army ever had. Course he had, you know, his staff under him that helped figure things out. They'd leapfrog these places, get established, and then give you a foothold and you didn't have all that slaughter on the beaches. That's the way we worked in New Guinea and that's the way it went all the way. But those poor bastards of Marines. They got the bloody jobs. Guadalcanal and Tarawa and places that were too small to leapfrog in. Just head in, that's all they could do. But New Guinea was huge. We could leapfrog and cut off the Japs and their supplies, too.

I was in the Pacific three-and-a-half years from New Guinea to the Phillipines. I couldn't count the landings we made. But we had it better than a lot of others. I can't complain. After the Phillipines we joined the Sixth Army and were slated for the invasion of Japan. But they had a rotation system by that time, and I had enough points to get a leave home. I wanted it. It had been a long time. This was the summer of '45 and I'd been out there since early '42. The war ended before we got to Seattle. So I never went back.

One time I'll never forget happened when we were fighting in Mindanao near a little town called Santa Maria. That place was full of scorpions and snakes, too. But it wasn't no desert. Your toes and fingers rotted. Spam turned black in an hour. Anyway, I was leading a patrol - I was platoon sergeant then - and this great big guy, a lieutenant from Texas, was with us in the middle of the patrol with the radio man. I had another very good sergeant as the back-up. The Japs would usually let part of a patrol go past their ambush, then hit. We wanted to make contact with the Japs near a hill where Joe Martin had got blowed up. We had a road block where the road branched around the hill and those Japs had a gun positioned on it. So we had to make contact. Find out what was what. We knew there was Japs on the hill. But where else?

So we're headed down this road. A shot goes off. We all take cover. Me and two other guys jump down into a little ditch. I land right on a bomb, about a hundred pound bomb that had wires running to it and a pin through the nose of it with rubber bands holding the wire to the pin. If that wire running off in the grass and bushes is pulled, that bomb would detonate. So we kind of sit there, me on the bomb, and we try to figure things out.

Off to the left I see something. I said, "Hey. That's a pill box?" We just sit there kind of steady. Them two guys was Keenan and Bracket. Bracket was from Boston. "We can see it," they says. "That wire goes right to it." So Bracket and Keenan just crawl out of the ditch and try to get around the pill box. I just stay on the bomb. I don't know whether to shit or go blind. Then that pill box opened up on those two guys. Keenan got up and started to run back toward the ditch and they shot him. He stayed down. I got out of the ditch, hit the dirt, and was trying to get over to Keenan. They opened up on me. I had two grenades and two water canteens on my belt and the damned canteens worked around to the front and I was crawling around with them under my belly and my butt up in the air - and they didn't hit me. I was working around toward Keenan, I thought. I see this grass moving ahead of me. I unpinned a grenade, but kept the pin. Then this big Texas lieutenant stands up in that grass, right in front of me. I yelled, "Hey, lieutenant!" He hit the ground, he rolled, and came to stop next to me. "Don't be calling me lieutenant out here," he says, and with Japs all around starts chewing me out. "They shoot officers first," he said. It's a miracle we wasn't both shot - or that I hadn't tossed that grenade.

I told him what had happened, and he went back to the radio man along the creek where there was a lot of cover. I stayed where I was a minute and this other sergeant came through the brush. He should have been killed, too. He says the patrol's took cover by the creek. I tell him Keenan's hit and maybe Bracket is both. And he says, "I'll see if I can find them." And so he starts off to hunt them. He was a good man. He should have been decorated, too. But I got the bronze star. He didn't get nothing except he didn't get killed. I sit there for a minute and hear a shot. Then this grass starts coming toward me with a little crack down its middle and it's Marx. We called him Harpo. He'd been shot in the arm. "I raised up," he said. "Thought I saw a Jap on the little knoll and I had and the bastard shot me." I told him to stay right there and I'd find the patrol and come and get him. So he did, and I went back to the creek and told the lieutenant, "Marx is up there and some others, I'll get Marx." So I brought Marx back. By that time another kid named Solomon worked up to where Keenan had been hit. Keenan was dead and Solomon raised him up and the Japs poured bullets into the corpse and killed Solomon, too. So there were two of them up there dead. Me and a Mexican kid named Jesus - we called him Sus - went looking for Bracket. I got up quite a ways and looked around. Sus hadn't followed me. I hollered, "Bracket, where are you?" I hear a voice off to my right. "Over this way." "Can you move?" I says. "No," he says. "Not without getting shot." I couldn't work over to him and drag him through. We'd have to raise up. I went back to the patrol and they radioed a cannon company and they poured fire into that area all night. As soon as the artillery fire began, we went in and got Bracket out.

We went up there the next day and the Japs had pulled out. They had a hell of a network of trenches back there. All those wires! They had bombs set up all over. Why they didn't trip them, I'll never know. They could have blowed us to kingdom come. We followed these wires out to these bombs and the demo guys took them apart. I found the one I'd set on.

So that was the operation they gave me a bronze star for. Usually you get in a mess and if you get out of it alive, they give you a medal. If you don't, they send you home in a sack and give your folks a purple heart.

No. I don't think much about the war any more. You know, if you lay in bed at night alone, you get to thinking about some of the things that are still a little spooky to you. But as far as bothering me, I don't think so. I think of some of the guys. But I was so damned glad to get home. I thought all that time if I ever get home, maybe I can lay down and go to sleep at night. And I sleep pretty good. But I didn't have it as bad as some people did, you know.

―――――

* * *

For me, the relationship between writing and teaching is a practical one. I was teaching (as we say, knowing you will modify the vanity) a lot before I wrote much; and for a long time now I have been teaching without writing much. But I was hired at Carleton because I had written some stories. That's what I mean by the relationship's being practical.

I wanted to teach long before I wanted to write. My ninth grade teacher in Plain City mentioned one day - we were out in the hall by the fountain - that he hoped I would someday join him in his vocation. He believed in vocation. I couldn't think of any reason why I shouldn't join him. I wrote nothing except school assignments - and you know what they are - until sloshing through Holland and Germany toward the end of World War II, I ran into some things that peeled me down to where the good words are. When I had time, I wrote some stories. Writing them was torture. Writing this is torture. Having written them was pleasant. Seeing them published and knowing they were read was bliss. Some of these stories were read by people at Carleton, and I was offered a job teaching literature and composition. Not fiction writing, the one thing I knew something about. I wanted certain assurances about graduate degrees. "One play of Shakespeare's is worth a library of dissertations," Larry, the Great Goulden Monarch, intoned for the ages in our living room in South Ogden. I quickly agreed, though I had a feeling we were off the subject. My stories had fled in a pack and were hiding outside in the oak brush, where they remained until He drove away.

All that was a long time ago. But even now I occasionally write a story or an essay. I, too, have committed a memoir.

Whether I would be a better teacher if I had written more, I do not know. Whether I would be a better writer if I had taught less, I do not know. If I had become a publishing critic/scholar, I would be somebody else and, therefore, a different kind of writer and teacher, and I think that would be too bad, for me.

A writing establishment exists in the schools that encourages the analysis of discourse and the teaching of writing and literature along highly sophisticated lines gathered from linguistics, the cognitive sciences, and modish political ideologies. The results of these inquiries and the debates generated by them are entombed in the professional journals, in a language so impervious to air and light that the pages could be used for the safe disposal of hazardous waste. Writing like this. . .

Well, that's mighty odd. I had a stack of College English *journals and they are gone. Just when I needed a specimen about to metastasize. In a Lethean fit, I must have thrown them out. But no matter. I carry with me a few allopathic samples. Theorists of literature, like theorists of composition, use language at the furthest possible distance from the quick of either physical or mental experience.*

> *"Together these broad thematic concerns suggest an overarching understanding of language and form as both agents of denial and agents of expression and an understanding of the complexity of linguistic response necessitated by personal traumas and cultural marginalization.."*

Another displaced person with vacant eyes joyously drones on about existing and potential totalities recognized "as already....relativized, temporal, centripetal entities in need of centrifugal destabilizing."

Something is wrong here, something too shallow for tears. Decent people go to school a long time to learn to write like that. A couple years ago in St. Louis at the CCCC meeting, an earnest young set of conditioned responses - his voice full of graduate fellowships and post-doctoral grants and cutting-edge solemnity - reminded me that this language is "...the voice of criticism and perfectly suited to the occasion." He had stated the matter exactly, and I suggested that with just a tad of concern about the quality of life, we could avoid such occasions. Our dialogue went nowhere. Pursuing the good life, I did not renew my long-held membership in the NCTE and its lamprey, the Conference on College Composition and Communication. We have to do what we can. If we can't beat them, we don't have to join them. No, we don't! We don't.

What makes good teachers and good teaching? I do not know. Whether writing of any kind or quality has anything to do with the matter is a mystery to me. Many fine teachers write little or nothing. Many not so fine teachers extrude volumes of plaster-board prose through their computers.

How about a few years' moratorium on all writing within academies, except for short pieces about frogs plopping into ponds and gentle rain falling through red, golden, and blue autumnal skies? If something beautiful, good, and true results, let the banana leaf speak of it first. In these parts, a burdock leaf will do.

Wayne Carver

SUSAN JARET McKINSTRY

THE KISS

Horses in a flooded field,
tufted new-green grass surreal
in the water-mirror,
stand like island mountains
against a storm-grey sky.
Hooves submerged, they perch
deerlike on delicate fetlocks,
grazing and drinking deep
at once.

What freedom! Each bite a sip, a chew,
no choice or movement necessary
to fulfill easy needs.
Heads down, tails to the wind
as they face identical eastward,
their coats alone are various -
dark, dappled, feathery with winter growth.

Their seasonal ease is not ours.
Predicting or mourning change,
wanting more or less of nature's provide,
we cursed the drought that dried the crops;
now the skies yield downpours
that drench us, the fields, and horses.
Slicker-clad, umbrella-shielded,
we groan, complain, ache for sun,
get faint consolation from spring sayings.
We wait for flowers.

Those horses hover,
graceful, self-contained, over
a transformed world. Earth erased,
they float on their own mirrored reflections
in a complete embrace,
tail tendrilling in the wind above
and in the water below,
belly to belly, shimmering in the faint disturbances,
lips touching lips in a nourishing kiss.

FISH STORIES

for Bob Tisdale

"You remember the one
that got away?
that summer? Well,
I could tell you stories."

A slow shake of the head, a wag of tongue,
a catch of recall.
"It was so hot the tomatoes cooked on the vine.
Flowers dried on the stem.
Birds stopped singing and fell down dead
from their dry nests.
Natural taxidermy.
And Silas and R. D. set out to catch the big trout -
you know the one - figuring there was no water to hide it.
They went on past Tucker's to the mill, and down to the stream.
But that fish fooled them. They couldn't even find the stream.
No trickle.   They gathered some bones and claimed they were
the earthly remains of the trout. Only confessed last winter.
That fish is still out there."

Recount, relive, revise; the embellished
productions of summer nights,
hooked on the recalled tellings of desire.
So myths are made. Creating the stories of summer,
time slowed to a breath of details -
a rocking chair, a turning fan, a sweating glass of lemonade.

Voices catch in the dusty air.
Words form pictures that dissolve with the drift of eyelids,
like whirling insects dazzling in the light of summer doorways,
the mysterious summons of fireflies,
the unmistakable bang of screen doors calling you back.
We cast lines to net the memory even as we live
the one that gets away -
the sting of blowing sand,
the instant nostalgia of song,
the unfolding events of a summer night.
These grow, in accounts, and then dry to paper
as the hot breath of imagination blows over them.

Bones are no proof of capture.

Recounting becomes another story,
another net of summer, another cast of tellings
that tide time into memory,
that shape our lives into spun stories
of what might have been, or could be, or even was.

STOPPING TRAINS

Flying, body horizonal
with a diver's certain faith
that space will end in water's welcome,
arms almost already reaching their goal,
lovefierce fingers stretched to stop hot speed,
like a child's cartoon hero, confident, just in time,
selfsleek and speedstrong, the woman
rages through air to get to the child
before the train does.
Clackety catastrophe rattling over cries,
a crushing embrace nearly there as she flies,
swoops in, sweeps child, stops train,
saves all that makes her life
a life.

Such moments fill a mother's dreams.
Her rage of love can in that sweep
of sleep turn waking terrors to salvation:
being always there in the fullness of time,
being selfseparate and still two with child,
being indeed Mother.
Stopping trains.

ELLEN LEARNING TO TELL: 1937

"Scheherazade must exercise her talent as a storyteller or die."
Gerald Prince, *The Study of the Narratee*

Voices sifted through the dark like fireflies,
Lighting on phrases that illuminated nothing.
"The only way" "there isn't enough" "we can't keep her."
The voices droned like insects, holding her sleepless
Through hot summer, through drifting fall,
Until night itself seemed hostile.

Day broke into the sullen story
Told everywhere those days, of need and want
Breaking families, making sacrifices of the flesh.
She was to go to other keepers,
The cost of her keeping paid out in small chores,
In company, in filling a silent house with sound.

She argued. She wept. Not better, she cried,
To be torn from family for food, when spirit may starve.
She embellished her claims, told of fantastic fears,
Transformed fairytales to find other ways to charm
The monster. Her voice wove through dinnertimes;
At night she lay awake, inventing new dreams for daylight.

She was sent to that cold house. The polished floors
Gave a self-satisfied echo, the walls gave no warmth.
Her starched room's silence kept her sleepless,
The droning family home gone so far from this dark,
The whisperings of grandmother, mother, tiny sister useless
Against all this glass reflecting no one.

She ate, dressed, worked, and felt herself foreign,
The kept thing, the unnamed guest-not-guest.
She began to tell stories to enchant her listeners,
Spin dreary details into tales to repay the bargain,
Until she could recount her dreamless days into anecdotes,
Dare her spirit to recast foundlings into family endings.

Like a bard for a king, she sang her days into ballads,
Paying the price for family, for keep, for worldgold
Out of her self-flesh, her mind's clothing richer by far
Than the plaids they provided, until the habit of telling
Became Scheherazade's prize, the story of her life, stories for love,
Stories she later gave her children as she wove them into her life.

CHASE

Children scatter before me
like leaves in harsh winds.
I am the monster mother here.
I chase to great delight.

Children taunt, "Get me!" "Get me!"
to tempt the monster's chase.
Trees, parents and swings are safe;
a circle of sidewalk the jail.

I fly at them, arms encircling
in a threatening hug.
I catch one, small fish wriggling
in the net of my careful grasp.

I carry it, small arms and legs
awhirl, and child heart pounding.
I jail it, but they swarm in glee
to free it when I turn.

I fly at them, arms encircling.
Some, just learned to walk,
toddle bowlegged in diapers, arms up
for balance and chase and embrace.

What if the monster was finally freed?
What if the chase was no game
but dread, swells of anguish, shrieks
not reclaimed to laughter?

Stress can snap stretched cable.
So nerves, skin-taut, can fray,
unravel the tightknit calm of play
into abortive rage.

The children know. They do not fear.
I am their monster mother here.
It is that risk they rush to,
and play for.

LEGACY

Deathbed battles in Victorian novels
recount grasping relatives, guarded secrets,
long-lost claims for love repaid
in legacies of revenge and reward.
Death turns out differently.
The treasure isn't money but memories,
and they remain tenaciously unpossessed.
"Remember the time -" we chant,
and then seek the thing that will fix
her words, our feelings, that moment
forever.

Snapshots stop time.
From a forgotten box in the basement,
dusty with mildew,
I take an 8x10 photo, black and white,
Christmas 1952.
Three generations: me, the fourth,
spending my last ten days in my mother's womb,
round as she sat between her sister and her mother,
her grandmother and her sons,
at a coffeetable decorated with a small Christmas tree,
coffeecups filled with crumpled napkins,
and a full ashtray balancing a burning cigarette.

My mother then
was the age I am now; I inherited
her cheekbones, faintly traced on Greatgrandma's jovial face
and sharply on my mother's, thin even in pregnancy.
My brothers, 2 and 5 years old, flank the couch
on Greatgrandma's oldest and Aunt Jane's youngest laps,
making faces at one another across that span of female relations.

I treasure that. But I was a stranger then,
not part of the moment held by that photo,
a memory of something I never knew -
an unbroken line of family,
daughters sharing children with mothers.

Now, a daughter, an orphan, a mother,
my legacy is the raincoat. Shapeless
when I pull it from my suitcase,
it fills with her form when I put it on - perfect fit,
our size the same until she shrank into illness.
I feel like her.
It was her suburban uniform
in all seasons of Chicago rain. I find
her business card, a crumpled dollar and a shopping list
in one pocket, Kleenex in another.

A private legacy, perhaps best of all:
showering back moments glimpsed before,
untreasured then for the very ordinariness
we seek through her leavings.
The raincoat's smooth brown arms enfold me in this Minnesota spring.
I pass a storewindow
and see, astonishingly, my mother's face
smiling in the rain.

DIVISIONS

It was the problem of the cat which always stopped her. She could figure out how to divide the linens and the pans, and even the silverware, but she didn't know what to do about the cat. It is always the material things that bind you, she mused as she pulled the soiled sheets from their bed - the wedding gifts and furniture and the picture on the bedroom wall you both like and want to wake up to every morning for the rest of your life.

She had been thinking of leaving him for years, since even before she married him. Never terribly decisive, she wavered for a year over whether or not to marry, and never really decided. Instead, she let the waves of reaction from her parents and his wash her through the wedding itself and even through the first months - not exactly blissful, but the doubts stayed quiet. It was some time before she recognized that she was again wondering whether or not to marry him, and she would stop, hands holding a soapy dish in midair, remembering with surprise that she already had. Lately as she was working around the house she found herself humming songs about aborted romances with an emphasis on Tammy Wynette's "D-I-V-O-R-C-E," even though she'd always hated country music. And she began to divide the household goods mentally, imagining the scene in which she and her husband would form two separate piles, his and hers, of all of those objects their marriage had collected. She was pleased with her decision and her action, after her years of drifting. To be stopped by a cat - that seemed unfair. She let that decision wait, hoping it would resolve itself somehow. After all, she thought, there's only so much one person can do.

"Joanna," he would call, "Where is my blue shirt?"

She would interrupt her inventory with a sigh and wander to the closet, giving the sticky left hand door on his side an extra jerk, and search through his shirts. He would stand close behind her, talking while her hands flicked through his clothes.

"Joe said Billings was really angry at the production department meeting Monday. I'm glad I was out of town. Did you read about the concert Friday? Do you want to go? I can meet you in the city after work. Joanna, are you listening? What are you thinking about these days?"

She turned to him, offering him the requested shirt and the slightly enigmatic yet sufficiently friendly smile she had spent an afternoon practising in the mirror. So far it had appeased him. He accepted the shirt, gave her a real smile in return, and left, calling back, "I'll find out about the tickets."

Safe, she went back to her work while she dreamed about the dividing, undoing those things that held them together, mentally removing plates from cabinets and posters from walls. The cat sat and watched her, eyes glinting.

"You've never kept the apartment so clean," he marvelled, and she smiled secretly, inspecting the house and possessions with a landlord's objectivity. She scrubbed each object, corner, sill as though she were preparing to move and wanted her security deposit returned in full, wanted to erase all signs of her tenancy. Everything had to be ready.

At night she lay thinking of the piles growing as she went over everything in the apartment, and she would fall asleep with a satisfied smile. Some nights he would come in while she was still awake, sorting, and touch her.

"Honey, does that feel good?"

An expression of distaste flickered across her face and she would quickly smile, trying not to meet his eyes. She would reach out to touch him, shifting until he could not easily reach her so she could stop trying to pretend to respond to caresses she hardly felt. Her eyes roamed over the objects in the room to see if their placement in his pile or hers had changed.

"You seem so far away, Joanna." She smiled, mentally saying goodbye to the mirror she had decided to let him keep.

"I love making love with you. I love you." Goodbye, clock whose alarm doesn't wake him up anyway. Goodbye, bedspread. He fell asleep with his head on her breast, breathing deeply while she counted through the night, ticking off objects. Often the cat lay across her feet and she tried to hate the dead weight of both of them, him and the cat, but the lights of a passing car would catch the cat's eyes in the dark and the glint made her start guiltily.

She dreamed that the piles she had so carefully made began to tremble and finally topple, sliding toward each other as she frantically tried to keep them separate, watching the mountains made up of thousands of careful decisions collide. Her cry woke him. As she started to tell him, she realized he couldn't know - not yet - and veered the dream into an on-the-spot nightmare about falling bookshelves.

"Now, you see how unreasonable that is, my tidy Joanna. Messy bookshelves won't hurt you. Go to sleep now. I'll hold you. Pleasant dreams, honey."

She cuddled into his arm and he slept while she lay, eyes wide in the darkness.

*

It was the 28th, and the inventory was done. Except for the cat. Joanna stalked about the apartment trying on anger as an approach, flinging his dirty underwear out the bathroom door to lie in the hall, kicking his dirty shirt into the corner of the closet reserved for laundry, picking up half-full beer cans and pouring the flat, sickly-sweet liquid down the drain. She tried to crush a can with one hand, but failed. The apartment neat, she sat down to wait. The cat watched her and, deciding she looked fairly settled, leapt to her lap and curled up, one paw over its nose. She scratched it idly and watched the hands on his mantle clock move too slowly. She felt the cat tense and turn its head to the door before she heard his key. He kissed her on the top of the head, his face flushed from the sultry air.

"Ninety-eight degrees already," he said. "Remind me not to play tennis again until September. How are you?"

"I'm leaving."

"I had an exhausting day. Had a meeting with Billings that lasted nearly three hours, and then lost my game with Joe. Can't beat his backhand." He flung himself into his chair, stretched out, shut his eyes.

"I'm leaving," she tried again. He didn't open his eyes.

"Oh, did you have something to do tonight? Sorry I'm so late. Do you have time for a quick dinner? I'll cook."

She took a deep breath. "I'm leaving you."

"God! It must be that time of the month again - you always qualify for the Scarlett O'Hara award then. Doctor Butler prescribes some good Southern home cookin'. C'mon, let's find some food."

She sighed and trailed behind him to the kitchen, watching while he leaned on the refrigerator door, checking the contents.

"I've already decided who gets what," she announced.

"Well, I hope I don't get the refrigerator because there's nothing in it." He gave her a jovial pat on the seat and began rummaging through the pantry.

"Didn't you hear me?"

"I heard you, honey." His voice came out accompanied by the sound of cans being moved around. "Peas, corn, peas, and parmesan cheese. God, there's no food in here!"

"You can keep the bed." She wanted to be generous.

"Thanks, Joanna, I am tired tonight and I've never liked sleeping on the floor. How about ordering a pizza for dinner?"

"Damn it, I'm talking about leaving you, and you want a pizza. Don't you care?"

"I care, Joanna." He stared at her a moment, then grinned and left the room, calling back, "But you won't leave. You love me. Besides, who'd get the cat?"

She heard the sounds of the phone dial, his voice ordering the pizza, her half cheese, his sausage, as usual. The cat rubbed against her leg briefly, then gazed at the food bowl. She opened the pantry door and, hands on hips, looked over the cans of cat food, different colors, flavors, brands, trying to decide which the cat would like. She selected "Gourmet Mix" and tried to avoid smelling it as she put it in the bowl and placed the bowl on the waxed floor. She squatted by the cat as it ate, running her hands over its sleek fur, pleased that it liked her choice. Perhaps after Christmas would be better. She could maybe get another cat before then and they could each take one. Christmas gifts would be easy to divide, and besides, she enjoyed his family during the holidays. Maybe she could go at the new year - that would be not only practical but symbolic. The cat purred as it ate, with an erratic, deep-throated gargle, and she crouched beside it until the pizza arrived.

*

* * *

I am an occasional writer in the fullest sense of the term: I write for the occasions in my life that I need to solve, to order, to recreate through words. The death of my mother and birth of my children demanded these very recent poems; the story is from my earlier **New Yorker** *phase, when seemingly the only subject for short stories was failing relationships, and I still like my odd, affectionate version. Now I seldom have time to finish any stories, although I invent children's bedtime stories, creation myths, lullabies and silly songs as a way of telling my children about the world. (When we drove past horses standing in a flooded field, 5-year-old Ryan's instant poem was "Horses in a flooded field/don't wear puddleboots/don't have raincoats/they don't care!" My version of that image is the poem entitled "Kiss"; I think his poem and mine have essentially the same meaning, though rather different narratives).*

Poetry, a sharply personal art, publicizes chaotic daily details into narrative order and shows us what events might mean. The writing process of telling stories teaches me what I need to learn, what listeners want to know, what words can tell us. That is why the tale of Scheherezade fascinates me. The link between living and telling, so dramatic in that story, indeed bridges our everyday lives from event to meaning. In writing, in reworking that link, I can retell a real event and give it a happier ending than it might have had, or create an event that answers my questions for me when no one alive knows the answer. ("Ellen Learning to Tell" is just such a poem. It grew out of a cheerful one sentence comment from my mother about learning, as a child, how to entertain listeners with anecdotes; after her death I learned that she had been sent away from home for a time after the Depression, and I puzzled out the possible connections between those events. Now I have invented the tone, the story, she never told; I suspect it is far from the "truth," but it answers my question).

Teaching narrative theory, studying the fictions of history, reading contemporary fiction, listening to students' stories, inventing literary answers to questions that derail me, I am awed by the multiple ways of telling the private creation myths we each need to get through the world, and the magic of those myths expressed in writing.

Susan Jaret McKinstry

KEITH HARRISON

HANDS

Here you are
Again, blunt spiders,
Both of you

Three legs short:
You scutter up smooth
Wood; you choke

Mop-handles.
Smart-asses, always
Acting for

Yourselves ! You
Clam up, rub bellies
Mindlessly

In sharp wind.
And why do you stroll
There, over

Sheets, hide in
Furred darkness under
My pillow ?

I don't know
You. Where are your eyes ?

SERIOUSLY

Soon we'll be
Gone from here, leaving
No traces

Save in our
Surest mimics - our
Kids' faces;

Truckloads of
Books, a few verses
That might stand

Fifty years
From now, and still sing.
Maybe not;

The wasted
Words will rot, with my
Snow-blasted

Trees, which are
Not mine anyway
I'm afraid.

Strange: I'm sure
I hurried back here
This time for

Something more.
But if you asked, *What
Was it* ? I'd

Say, *That's tough.*
I'm like a man who's
Left something

Important
Upstairs, but watches
Three starlings

Jibbering
On the lawn. I guess
I forgot

What's up there;
The birds beguiled me -
Though I'm still

Looking for
That serious thing -
But not, it

Now appears
(And might well be) quite
Seriously.

THREE LOVE POEMS FROM THE JAPANESE

Thinking of him again,
I dozed off.
But when he climbed
Into my bed
I made a mistake:
I opened my eyes.

*

The autumn wind
Rasps my body.
And I depend on her
As night
Depends on night.

*

When I think of her
Too much
I put on my bed-clothes
Inside out.

THANK YOU, PYTHAGORAS

This little
Varying dance of
Threes and five

Fits me well;
It keeps my flatfoot
Wits jumping;

It can flick
Fast as a tomtit's
Tail - or move

Extremely
Slow, like mauve seaweed
Pulsing in

A green sea.
Here, one small word can
Swell, to a

Landscape wide
As Minnesota,
Or even

Wider - say
To the blind dark of
Milton's Hell.

A certain
Mathematical
Imp or spell

Hides in it.
Most anything goes
Within its

Free confines:
Pop, be-bop, jumped up
Reggae bump

Bums against
Karlheinz Stockhausen
And Berio.

If Dante,
Instead of terza
Rima, had

Found this thinned
Down version, he would
Have wet his

Pants. Just think
Of the eyes saved - and the
Printer's ink !

FIVE   SEASONS

Morning flares
In the curtains. Quick,
Wake up, take

Me now. I
Will be ravished in
Lilac-light !

Faster than
A shot pellet, or
Sprung slingshot,

A sharp bird
Stabs an apricot.
The rot starts.

Flies doze on
On a burnt rose, dreaming
Of garbage

Crystals in
Their huge eyes glow like
Church windows

Green burns down
In urns of burnished
Umber gold

As if a
Sultan's roof turned to
Copper flames.

Icicle ?
Tooth of a god ? Don't
Think, snap it

Off the spout !
Feed it, quick, to the
Stove's red mouth.

FOUR SONGS FOR CHILDREN

It Just isn't Fair

Because I ate three Eskimos for tea
And seven sausages and half a pie
When Mum came home from work she yelled at me
And both my greedy sisters began to cry:

'He's always doing things like that', they said.
They dragged me to my room and yanked my hair.
My brother poured old dog food on my head.
I tell you, in this house it isn't fair.

Tonight when they're asleep I'll boil the phone.
I'll nail my brother's trousers to the telly -
And in the morning, won't my sisters groan
When all their teddy bears are dressed in jelly.

Oenone's Jingle
or *Do You Like These Words I Just Learned Them Today ?*

Daddy, I love you Deliberately,
And Mummy, I love you Definitely too,
If birds had wings they'd Scriffle past me
And I'd call this house the Potbelly Zoo.

I'd give them names like Doctor's Pointment
Nile Crocodile and Curring Cough;
I'd rub their teeth with Purple Ointment.
That's Twenty Eighteen. And that's enough !

Where Do Birds Go ?

Where do birds go when they sleep ?
        Into the dark, like prayers.
Keep very still and you can hear
        Their heart-beats on the stairs.

Where do dogs go when they stop ?
        They dive into their bones
Forget their tongues, rub off their skins
        And doze in the quiet zones;

They wait a thousand thousand years
        And then came barking back
As if they never died at all
        To pee on my grocery sack.

How many cats patrol the dark ?
        One great Cat, one only.
With flaming eyes he roams the world -
        So sleepless, and so lonely.

I and Franko

How would you like a galoshes breakfast ?
        No thanks, Franko, I broke my tongue.
Bet you can't catch a passionfruit grapefruit -
Bet you never heard of a - clapperbung.

        Listen, Franko - you're always yakking
        And yukking, and cracking your toes,
        Why don't you wash your head in a bucket -
        I don't care if your nose gets froze.

                Franko got mad - he stole my bike,
                He took Dad's Volvo out of gear.
                Dad ran out, shouting 'Spifflicate !'
                Bye, bye Franko - see you next year.

113

SNAKE TIME

Drove up here
Forty years ago,
Remember

How, at dawn
In the smokey light
I saw the

Tiger-snake
Stretched out, there, on the
Tar, rising

At me, fast:
Stood up, terrified,
Braking hard:

If my wheels
Flick him up, over
My back, he'll

Bite my neck !
Too late. My tires bump
His back-bone,

And I wait.
Nothing. Already
Many wheels

Had ruined him:
His bright striations
All ripped and

Bloodied, he
Lay there, receding
In my mind.
And was it
Five miles back, I passed
A struck roo

Dreaming on
His side - a big grey,
Sung by flies ?

I pull up.
I look all around.
Nothing moves.

Grass whitens
In the migraine heat,
The same dead

Ghost-gums on
The singed hill-top crack
Without sound.

Drive on. Time
Is the queerest place
We live in.

EVEN STEVENS

Kelpies dodge
Between their pup-yaps
And last bones

But even
Last bones aren't final:
Sun-whacked, they

Break up and
Blossom in wheat or
Thistle-spikes.

This is our
Damnation: never
Getting there;

Also our
Only paradise -
As Stevens

Reminds us
Paradoxically,
In live words

That stay there
Fixed on the page - e.
g. *blackbirds.*

SINGLE HANDED

Here is a man examining his hands under a hurricane lamp, which he has just lit with great difficulty, after crashing in from the lake, yelling *OH, JESUS !* then, after a pause, *OH, JESUS, WHAT IS THIS !*

He needs to look very closely because, embedded between the knuckles of the little finger and the ring finger of his left hand, is a large fish-hook. The barb is stuck through the back of his hand and pointing upward through the palm.

The person who did this to him can't help because he is lying on the floor of the dinghy from which they'd both been fishing. It happened like this: Merle, his partner, had had a strike, very close to the boat, from a huge muskie and had tried, with all his force, to set the hook immediately, but the hook had torn out of the fish's mouth and into *his* hand instead and now it is really set. In the confusion that followed, Merle - an old man - had slipped over backwards and struck his head on a metal thwart, and right now he is either unconscious or dead.

One further trouble: he had been fishing with a single hand anyway because the other is thickly bandaged, and splinted, because of an accident at the dock two days ago.

By rowing around in half-crazy circles with one oar through the cross-currents, he somehow got the boat back to the dock and made Merle, or Merle's body, as comfortable as he could, and then cut the metal leader from the hook by holding his fish-knife between his boots and sawing at it for so long and with so little effect that he was surprised when the metal stands eventually weakened and snapped.

Now he is staring at his hands, wondering how he managed to light the lamp - but that hardly matters.

He knows there are some pliers somewhere in the shed, but it takes him a clear half-hour to find them. By that time the lamp is out and he has to re-fill it and re-light it. Another twenty minutes, and night thickening everywhere. And Merle, dead or living, must be getting cold.

He stands up, too abruptly, to listen to the sound of an outboard on the lake, and knocks the lamp over, and everything goes black save for a thin slice of moonlight through the porch doorway. He fumbles for the pliers with his right elbow and his hooked hand; finds them, then angrily kicks the door open. The moonlight widens and he squats down in it. Now he tries to get one foot between the handles of the pliers, and the other on top of the upper handle. At the same time he has to slide the barb of the hook into the mouth of the pliers, and press the top foot down, slow and hard. He wants to cut the barb off clean, and draw the shank of the hook back through his hand.

But the pliers turn over, and his hand with them. The pain explodes from the center of his palm and suffuses his whole body. It is so overwhelming that he doesn't say anything at all. He is sure now there is no one listening. He tries again. And again. And once again. And fails.

He leans back against the wall of the porch, and listens to the loons somewhere out there in the night.

This will be a helluva story when it's over. Merle will be dead, or alive. He himself will be dead from sepsis, or alive - with a beer in his hand - telling someone about it, maybe Merle.

He reaches for the pliers and decides to try the same trick again.

It's the only trick he knows.

BARRACOUTA FISHERMAN, TASMANIA
from Australian Tongues

You have to get up early, be five miles off the coast as dawn comes up over the headland. That's the best time. No one knows why. Maybe the small fish rise to the light and the big ones follow, or maybe they're hunting water-lice. Who knows ? Anyway, they're always just under the surface, about half a meter down. So you take the jig-stick and you thrash the water behind the stern like a madman and sometimes while you're flailing away and all the water's white you hook one in the gills or the belly and it feels like you've got a bull on the end of your wrist.

And specially when the wind's heaving white caps all around and you hit a school. You've got six lines out and the boat's like a guitar trailing its strings through the water. Suddenly all the strings go tight at once and you see a little fleck of foam on the end of each line, dancing on the water, and you have to haul the fish in against the run of the boat. Bloody hard work. And you can't stop pulling because the jig doesn't have any barbs on the hook. You gotta keep the pressure steady right up to the boat then swing him up out of the water into the tank then flick the jig back fast. One movement, and when the line snaps taut you start hauling again.

Last week we worked like that - three hours in a single school and I remember thinking what a terrific sound it'd make if you could pluck all the strings at once, and the whitecaps bobbing and the wind howling. *Jesus, it was beautiful !*

It's up and down a' course but it's a livin. I been round 'couta boats since I could walk. Built this one last year, every plank. You know, when you rub your hands against a boat you built yourself, it's like a living thing, and last night we were coming down the estuary near dusk and all around the boat there was this green fire in the water-weed and I looked up at the light falling behind the island and it all seemed old - as if you were seeing it again for the first time and it was all ending, or maybe it was all beginning.

LEGS

For my students

How many one-legged soldiers have marched for two-legged kings ?
Look at them hopping across the screen, black suits
Pressed for Remembrance Day, medals from Vimy Ridge and
Passchendaele
Banging against their chests, and the film jumping to the rhythm
Of their crutches. There are enough to fill five cities;
And even on single legs they keep faithful step, eyes fixed as bayonets
Dead ahead.

How soon they forget that the king has dressed himself in a score
Of counterfeit uniforms all bloodied now, and stiff, under a song of
flies.
Meanwhile the king, in a long frock and feathered hat, surveys the
campaign
From a distant manor, advisors swirling around him
With maps as he smooths the expensive silk
Along his thighs.

At this, and any time, not to be paranoid
Is highest foolishness. This executive, whose eyes
You cannot see behind his brilliant lenses, will never hack your hands off;
He will take what dreams in you on the twentieth floor at coffee-break -
The part that shapes a tune for your flute, or bends a clay bowl
To the exact form of your delight - and he will tweezer it out of you
Very slowly.

See them milling there in the quadrangle, these youngsters
Ready to be crippled for someone else's dream of excellence
Which carries them to a high apartment above the wrinkled river,
An apartment blank as Hotspur's eye as he stares up at the cold clouds
Riding over.
                    Meanwhile the young pretender struts about
Building his kingdom on the skull-bones of his father; and once
At twilight, alone in the royal ante-room, he slips the crown
Over his curls, listens to his father's sick breathing
And smiles into the mirror.

His name is Hal, and he is everywhere.

Watch him, I tell you.
Go well downriver, build a small shack on the tidal flats
Camouflaged like an egret's nest so the black
Patrol boats can't pick you out with their long
Eye-beams at midnight.

Hunker down, be suspicious of any communique which offers
Terms for your surrender.

* * *

When lack of time doesn't put them on a collision course, the arts of writing and of teaching are mutually re-inforcing because they have so much in common. Human beings, like words, are unpredictable, surprising, sometimes recalcitrant, and always a test for the wits. Beyond that, literature is the most incarnate of the arts because a story or a poem is something that happens in our toes, our throats, our bloodstream; when we are at our best it's as if everything that's in us wants to speak or sing.

And teaching is a wholly human art too. There seem to be three major philosophies about teaching: the subject-centered, the teacher-centered and the student-centered. A nice academic distinction, and O.K as far as it goes. What it misses is that true teaching is a genuine exchange, a dialogue in which human beings share something of the fullness and richness of the world we try to live in.

And, when we write, the language is like a person: we have to treat it with respect, talk to it, argue, listen, learn when to interfere and when to leave off. Timing is everything, and it's always chancy. Just when we have learned something about one aspect of either craft, the whole situation changes - a new class, a formal problem we didn't look for - and here we are, a student, an apprentice once again.

I have sometimes told my students (I am not all sure they believe me) that writing doesn't get any easier with time because the human brain has some daemonic or angelic propensity to keep on inventing problems which are just beyond its reach. We are always beginning. It's interesting, and frightening, to think what life would be like without such carrots.

As a fledgeling teacher I thought I might be able to give the world a little nudge here and there. If I've learned anything at all since then it's that, if one does succeed in nudging the world, the will has very little to do with it. Luck has a lot. But luck is not a simple matter. When the poet John Frederick Nims was here a while back, he told the students, rather cryptically, that Beethoven made absolutely no contribution to Economic Theory. What he meant, I think, was that, for Beethoven, luck had no room to move in that realm. When he sat down at the piano, which he did for hundreds of hours, it did. And it wasn't only a matter of talent. He had to sit down at the piano.

I suppose that's the rub: we have to learn to work, and when to work, and when to wait. And if we can get all that right, something else might be able to get on with the nudging.

Keith Harrison

JANE TAYLOR McDONNELL

RADICAL INNOCENCE

I am standing in front of the theatre marquee in our small town. It is seven o'clock in the evening and the lights are flickering rapidly. I am holding the hand of a two year old boy, my son, who stands entranced by the lights, fixated, hardly moving. Each night at seven he has to come to watch them and I bring him willingly, cheerfully explaining to our friends as they enter the theatre why I am there, how much he loves these lights. At first I see nothing strange in this. Paul loves lights. He turns them off and on for hours each day. He knows where every light switch is in our house and the houses of our friends and in many of the stores down town. His world is lights and light switches.

I remember another scene. Two years earlier. In the delivery room, we watch the first moments of this new baby. Taken up in a bundle of loose blankets, he is placed on the warming table. Crying, rolling vigorously from side to side, he kicks, breaks free of the folds of the blanket and opens his eyes. Most newborns that I have seen are curled in on themselves, as if they need to fold themselves away from the onslaught of the world for fear it be seen too soon, too suddenly. Not this one. This baby seems to open his eyes to the full sense of things all at once. Eyes opened wide, he stops crying and stares at the lights on the ceiling. "He's a keeper," exclaims the attending nurse, and in my new mother's egotism, this seems like a wonderful omen. I think I have never seen such sudden sense, such full startled awareness, such awakening to the world.

A third scene. Paul, two and a half at the time, is sitting on the floor of the kitchen, with his back to us as we work around the stove roasting a chicken for dinner. Jim speaks to him by name. No response. Paul doesn't turn around or indicate in any way that he hears us. Jim calls him again by name. Again no response. And again and again, until in utter frustration, Jim shouts at him, "You dummy!" and drops the chicken on the floor. It falls out of the pan and slides in its grease all the way across the floor. We eat dinner in angry silence, feeling as if we have broken through some membrane of consciousness and are face to face with something neither of us is ready to face--a child who unaccountably doesn't even know his own name at the age of two.

When did we begin to worry? Later, I often looked back over these early months, searching for sign-posts that may have been missed at the time. But even when we did begin to worry our complaints were vague. We took him to his pediatrician when he was ten months old. We had small complaints, hardly formulated. "He seemed slow to develop gross motor skills, but not very slow." "He was content to sit in one place." "He didn't explore the world the way another child did

123

who was born on the same day." We worried, but felt guilty about worrying, as if we shouldn't. The pediatrician sent us away with a reassurance that failed to reassure. "You aren't raising a race horse," he pointed out--a comment that stung.

We spent Paul's first summer in France and England, and should have been very happy. I have a picture taken at this time: June 1973, our garden on the edge of the little village of Contignac, in the south of France. Paul, at ten months and just learning to stand, is holding onto one side of a metal lawn chair. My seventy year old father, who has come with us to babysit while we both write our dissertations, stands on the other side of the chair. He is watching Paul. He has just taken a pebble from the corner of Paul's cheek. The sun comes through the green leaves of the lime trees; it shines through the wispy blond curls at the baby's neck. Both faces have a look of open innocence.

Every morning at this time my father takes the baby down the hill to greet an old man. This old man belongs to the farming family just down the lane and he is put out by his daughter to sit all day by the side of the road or, if it is raining, in the mouth of the mushroom cave. My father speaks no French; the old French man, who is deaf and senile, speaks no English. But with the baby, together they communicate. For them it is enough.

Looking at that picture now, I want to pick up the baby, to re-enter that time. I want to blow kisses through his silky hair, to plant them on his small hard skull. I didn't know then the fragility of that moment, over which already the dark wing was passing. I didn't know, and wouldn't know for another fifteen years, that the brain cells were clumping differently at the base of that little skull, that, wrapped around the cerebellum, the cisterna magna was enlarged.

During this summer, I repressed my worries, but I continued to notice things. In a restaurant in our little town, we put Paul on the floor to crawl at our feet. Another baby, there with its parents, was also placed on the floor. They were the same age, but the little French baby crawled around Paul, around and around, as he just sat there, in his little peaked sun cap with fish hanging from the crown. They babbled together, and the French couple pointed out that now their sounds were the same, but soon they would be differentiated as they learned their respective languages.

Paul's babblings did not become differentiated, however. He did not start to imitate the sounds he heard around him; he did not begin to speak English. In Cambridge, later that summer, where he had his first birthday, I showed him the lights in our rented house, switching on and off the light in the hallway, showing him how to make it work and saying over and over: "light, light." He appeared to comprehend, looking from the light to the switch, to my mouth, as I formed the word. He reached for the light, opened his mouth, made sounds, seemed to try to form the right sound. A friend commented that "light" has been the first word of so many babies, and it seemed so appropriate to us, so fundamental: *In the beginning there was light.* We remembered his wonder at the light on the delivery room ceiling and thought surely this would be his first word also.

It seemed that he was about to say "ight," "ight!"   Later, I wondered if it was just my imagination that he seemed so very close to speaking, so comprehending and ready for communication. Language was there. And then it was just out of his reach.

In fact, language was to remain out of his grasp for another year and a half, until he was two and a half. During that time, he seemed not to know that he had a name or that we had names. There was no "mama" or "dada." He did not point for a long time, he never asked for what he needed by trying to make sounds. He did not understand that sounds had meaning or that they could be used deliberately and could help him gain some control over his world.   He seemed not to communicate in other ways.

Looking back later, we realized other things were different. In Cambridge, Paul began to explore his world, but with a difference. He learned to climb the stairs of our rented house, a very "typical," "normal" activity for an eleven month old baby. At the top of the stairs, the first time he climbed them, he patted the floor. Following him, I also patted the floor.   He patted the floor more loudly and enthusiastically. I did the same. After that, every time he climbed the steps, he patted the floor on the same spot before he moved on. Then he took the same path each time past the toilet, where he looked in fearfully at this thing that made so much noise, then the bathroom.

At the top of the steps, he never omitted the pats, nor did he ever turn right instead of left. He never climbed the steps to get to his room-- which was just at the top of the stairs on the right and where there were toys, nor did he move on to explore our room further down the hall. He was able to crawl outdoors to the garden in back, but he invariably went to the same spot -- a small stake at the edge of the asparagus patch. There, he would haul himself up and hang on that stake, laughing and shouting, where he knew we could always count on finding him whenever he disappeared from the house.

Over the next year, between the ages of one and two for Paul, we felt more and more anxious. His pediatrican suggested that I was "doing too much for him, not giving him a chance to ask for things for himself." So one day I withheld a banana from him, as he sat in his high chair. I knew he was hungry. I held the banana just out of reach, saying clearly over and over, "banana, banana," then adapting and playing with baby sounds, "ba ba ba, ba ba ba."

I thought, "if I get any kind of sound out of you, I'll give it to you. Just open your mouth. Say something. Anything!" Paul became more and more agitated, squirming in his chair, bouncing up and down, reaching for the banana, watching my mouth, trying to say something, struggling to speak.

Finally he burst into tears. He fell back in the chair and sobbed. He sobbed in the most abandoned tones I had ever heard from him. Feeling guilty about my own behavior and angry at the doctor, I picked him up and held him close against my shoulder. I gave him the banana, and swore I would never, ever try this particular experiment again. It seemed so clear to me at that moment that he was trying to speak, trying to give me what I wanted. It was also crystal clear that he couldn't.

* * *

Radical Innocence is part of a longer work on my autistic son and on the experience of being his mother. I had lived for sixteen years or so with something that nothing - not my upbringing, not my education, not any amount of reading or talking - could have prepared me to understand. For those years, I lived in the presence of a different way of thinking, a different way of being in the world. And I began to want to give that 'difference' voice.

The autistic child has only knowledge, never imagination, hypothesis, intuition, belief, pretence. The willingness to entertain possibility just for the pleasure of it, the 'let's pretend' of his younger sister, were utterly foreign to my son as he was growing up. And so my task, in this book, was to try to translate across a borderland, to give voice to a different way of being human, one with its own courage and integrity. In this book I make up the stories that will give shape to what will probably always remain for me unknowable.

Writing is a way of reaching for something which cannot be known, except in the telling of it. But writing is also a way of constructing the self, of becoming a certain kind of self. This kind of writing, non-fiction, autobiographical, contemplative, sometimes seems particularly exposed, particularly risky. But, like the feminist classes I teach, it affirms certain values. It reminds me that the mothering women do, have done historically, is not merely instinctive, but a way of thinking. And it reminds me once again that the self is formed through relationships, through engagement with others, never just in isolated meditation.

Jane Taylor McDonnell

GREGORY BLAKE SMITH

HANDS

Here in New England we sit in chairs.

It's from my porch rocker that I watch the raccoon. He usually comes at dusk, that time of day half dog and half wolf, when the downturned leaves seem to glow with the sunset and the upturned ones glimmer with moonlight. I watch him pad through autumn weeds while the sweat of my chairmaking dries on my skin. He lingers in the shadows, still woodside, the sun falling further with each moment, and then waddles onto my lawn. He looks like an overgrown house cat once the woods are behind him. He tosses a wary look at me and then slowly disappears behind the chair shop. After another minute I hear the enormous crash of my garbage can lid falling on the stones. He doesn't even bother to run off as he used to, dawdling at the wood's edge until it's safe to come back. He seems to know I won't leave my chair.

"A twenty-two," my neighbor Moose says while I pare stretchers. "A twenty-two and then we won't blow the b'Jesus out of the pelt."

I take a few more cuts with my gouge and then ask him how he thinks the raccoon missed his trap line all this time. He peers at me with that cold menace of old age. He has a white beard that rims his chin like frost.

"It probably don't run my way," he says. "But if you want it trapped I can trap it. It's just a pissload easier to shoot it if it's coming every night like you're ringing the dinner bell. Right here," he says and he goes over to the window just above my workbench and taps at a pane. His fingers are scarred with patches of old frostbite. "We'll take this here pane out. I can rest the barrel on the mullion. If it's close enough I'll get it clean through the head and I'll be richer one pelt and you'll be poorer one dinner guest."

I tell him I'm not sure I want to kill him.

"*Him* ?" he says. "How d'you know it's a *him* ?" And he spits on my woodstove so the cast iron sizzles.

Outside, my moaning tree sends up a regular howl.

"*Please* cut that tree down, Smitty," my sister Jaxxlyn says every weekend when she comes up from New York. "It's driving me positively psychotic."

I tell her it's a·poplar. I can't cut it down. I don't use poplar in my chairs.

"But you heat with wood," she says. "Don't you? Don't you heat with wood?"

Not poplar wood I don't, I say. Too soft.

"It's driving me positively psychotic, Smitty."

I say what about New York. What about the car horns and the sirens. She says they don't have trees that moan in New York, Smitty. Smitty, she says.

My name is Smith. I'm a chairmaker with a tree that's grown itself tight around a telephone pole and a raccoon that's taken a fancy to my garbage. I've never minded the name Smith. I like the ancestral whiff of fashioning and forging in its single syllable. And I don't mind the moaning tree and its outrage over the telephone poles that have been stabbed like stilettos into the landscape, rubbing its insulted bark in the slightest breeze and howling when the wind blows in earnest. But the raccoon has unsettled me and I don't know why. My sister - who hates her last name and is being driven psychotic by my moaning tree - is not bothered by the raccoon.

"I think he's *cute*," she says, sitting on my porch with me as the fat creature moves from shadow into moonlight and back into shadow. "My friend Flora in the west seventies has a skunk for a pet. You should see him, Smitty! His little claws go clack-clack-clack on the linoleum, you know? Of course he's been desmelled or whatever they do to them. Oh, Smitty!" she says as the garbage can lid crashes on the stony ground. "Isn't that the cutest thing? How does he do it? Just *how* does he do it? Do you leave the lid on loose for him? Is that how he does it?"

Hands, I tell her, and I feel a faint panic at the word. They've got hands. And I hold my own hands up in the gloom, the backs reddish with dusk, the palms silver with moonlight.

When Monday comes I try tying the lid shut with mason's twine. That night there is no aluminum crash and I think: so much for hands, so much for raccoons, so much for half dog and half wolf! The next day I start in on a set of eight Queen Anne chairs, carefully designing the *S*-shaped legs to Hogarth's line of beauty. But that evening the raccoon comes trotting along the forest floor, hiking up onto my lawn behind the shop. It takes him a few minutes longer, but eventually the harsh, bright crash shatters the dusk. I sit in a stupor. In ten minutes he emerges from behind the shop. He pauses partway to the wood's edge and tosses me a scornful look over his shoulder and then vanishes into the now-dark bushes.

"You might open up a motel," Moose suggests, "seeing as what you already got yourself a restaurant."

My cabriole legs aren't right. I can't strike the balance between knee and foot. It's never happened like this before. I get out Hogarth's *Analysis of Beauty* and look his *S*'s over, and I print *S S S S S* on my graph paper, write my own name: *Smith, Smith, Smith, Smith,* but when I go to draft my Queen Anne leg I can't balance the knee to the foot, the foot to the knee, the *S*'s top orb to its bottom. I spend a whole day at my drafting table, trying, and end up tossing a sheaf of rejected legs into the stove. That night the raccoon dines on pumpkin and old cantaloupe.

* * *

If I can't work I'll hunt wood, do the felling now and wait until the first decent snow to find the marker ribbons and sledge the logs out with Moose's snowmobile. I plan on a two-day roam, bringing my sleeping bag and some food. At the sight of my bucksaw, my moaning tree groans.

I'm going to forget about raccoons.

I poach my lumber, and maybe that's why I have a feeling of trespassing when I go into the woods, of being where I only half belong. There are stone walls everywhere, built in earlier centuries and now running mute and indecipherable through the forest. Walking, I try to picture perfect S's in the air, but the stone walls distract me. They are like hieroglyphs on the land. From time to time I come across an old foundation, a sprinkle of broken glass in the weeds and a small graveyard a ways off. I find a bottle or two, an old auger, but they look as alien there as I do. Further on, the stone walls are so tumble-down they have ceased to look like walls. There is a feeling of low menace all around.

I mark my wood as I go, but on this trip I keep my eyes open for hollowed trees, for trees with holes, a cicatrix, disease. I climb up several and look inside, peer up the trunk of one, but there's no sign of habitation. That night, lying on dark pine needles, I have a recurring picture of the raccoon back at my house, sitting at the kitchen table in one of my chairs, with knife and fork in hand - perhaps a napkin - eating.

By noontime on the second day I've swung around to where I know there's a stand of tiger maple near a marshy pond two miles from the house. I spend the afternoon carefully harvesting the rare, figured wood, dragging the delimbed trunks down to the pondside and stickering them off the ground so they won't rot. The work puts the raccoon out of my mind. I feel healthy, feel the steel teeth of my bucksaw sharp and vengeful, the rasp of the sawn wood like the sound of defeat. But after the last haul, just as I sit content and forgetful on a stump, I catch sight of a tiny footprint on the soft silt that rings the water. Further on, there's another one.

There's a hush over the pond. The marsh reeds stand like pickets along the shore. Across the way the shadows between the junipers and low laurels seem to breathe in and out. I have a feeling of having been tricked, of having been watched all along. On the water the whirligigs hover like spies. A scarlet leaf flutters through the blue air and lands a foot or so from the raccoon's footprint, then cartwheels slyly until it covers the print. But it's too late. In the west, where my house is, the sun is kindling nests of reddish fire in the blue tops of the spruces.

You've got yourself a comfy den, I'm saying half an hour later after I've found the raccoon's beech tree. I've brought a crotched branch from the pondside for a leg-up, and I'm peering into a yawning hole maybe ten feet off the ground. I say it out loud. I do. I say: leaves and dried reeds, decaying wood for heat, some duck down. You've done all right. Yes, you have. You've done all right.

The trees seem to stir at the sound of my voice. I pull my head out and listen. They sound baffled, outraged. I want to say to them: "Do you think so? Do you think so? So *I'm* the intruder ? Do you think so?" But I don't. I just look at the hasty illogic of the shadows. Trees don't come on all fours and pry your garbage can lid off, I say. Even Darwin can't see to that, I say, and I go back to looking inside the raccoon's den.

I'm not afraid he's in there somewhere. I *know* what time of day it is. I *know* where he is. But off to the side, in a decaying burl, something has caught my eye, something shiny and unnatural. I look closer and realize he's got himself a cache of junk, bottle caps and aluminum can rings. Then in the next instant I recognize a piece of old coffee cup I'd broken in the summer, and then too a router bit I'd chipped and thrown out, then an old ballpoint, a spoon, screws.

Are you a user of spoons too, raccoon? I finally say out loud. And screws? And pens? Are you a writer of sonnets? I say.

But even as I talk I hear footsteps behind me on the leaves. I pull my head out and look around, but there's nothing moving, just the vagrant leaves falling. I listen again, hear them coming closer. Is it the raccoon returning? I hang fire a moment and then start hurriedly down the trunk. But before I do I reach in and steal back my old ballpoint. I hide the crotched limb in some bushes nearby.

* * *

For the next few days I wonder just how much the raccoon knows. There's no new contempt evident in his regard as he bellies up out of the woods onto my lawn - but he may be a master of his emotions. Jaxxlyn has put a bowl of water out for him. She says she's going to move it nearer to the house each day until the raccoon gets used to being with us. She wants me to do the moving on the weekdays.

My West Hartford client calls and asks how her Queen Anne chairs are coming. I start to tell her about the raccoon. I start to tell her about William Hogarth and beauty and order, about how a man can't work when a raccoon's eating his garbage, about how I've allowed

Violence! I spit through my teeth, stumbling back through the woods. I don't even try to staunch the blood coming from the punctures on my wrist. *Violence! Violence!*

* * *

Moose laughs. He laughs and asks how much the first of my rabies series costs. I'm sitting in his living room feeding bark into his stove. I don't answer him at first. I'm sick and I ache from the shot. Finally I tell him twenty dollars.

"Well, let's see," he says and he sights down the barrel of his twenty-two. "A raccoon pelt brings thirty dollar nowadays. You already used up twenty of them dollars on that shot. But I figure my half is still fifteen. So I figure you owe me five dollar."

I muster enough character to tell him he's getting a little ahead of himself, he's getting a little eager.

"No eagerer than that raccoon's getting," he says. The frostbite on his face crumples with his laugh, as if the skin there were half alive. I sit sullen and witless. I feel wasted. I don't know what to do. The raccoon comes and ravages my garbage.

I lie in bed for two days. When I'm up again I ask Moose for one of his box traps. I tell him I don't want to shoot the raccoon, I want to trap him. And once I've trapped him I want to let him go. He looks at me like this is confirmation of some suspicion he's had about me all along, never mind raccoons, some suspicion he'd had since he met me and my chairs.

"I ain't altogether sure a raccoon will trap so near a house," he says. "Raccoons ain't dumb."

This one will, I say. He's a modern raccoon.

But that night, sitting in my warm chair shop on a half-finished Queen Anne chair, I watch the raccoon stop and inspect the trap, puff at the acorn squash inside and then waddle over to the garbage can. He knocks the lid off with a professional air, but before he crouches into the garbage, he tosses a disdainful look through the windowpane at me and my chair. Behind him the trap sits in a state of frozen violence.

Beauty is the visible fitness of a thing to its use, I say to the raccoon in my dreams. Order, in other words. In a Puritan voice he answers back: "Not entirely different from that beauty which there is in fitting a mortise to its tenon."

I wake in a sweat. My wound itches under its bandage.

On the second night, kneeling on the wooden floor in my shop, the chairs empty behind me, I watch the raccoon sniff a moment longer at the squash but again pass it up. This time it's contempt in his face when he catches sight of me through the windowpane. That night the air turns cold.

eagle's claws for chair feet in the past, lion's paws too. But this raccoon is asking too much, I tell her. There's a silence on the line when I stop - and then she asks again how her chairs are coming.

"Six inches each day," Jaxx tells me as she gets into her car. "Six inches, Smitty."

Monday I can't work. Tuesday I can't either. Tuesday evening I wander off into the woods again, walk the two miles to the raccoon's tree. Somewhere on the way I know we cross paths. Is he hiding from me? I get the crotched limb out of its hiding place and steal back a screw.

The next morning I get the mating *S's* of the cabriole legs down perfectly in ten minutes, and by sundown I have all sixteen legs squared up and cut. That night I take the router bit back.

Thursday it's another screw. Friday a piece of china. I'm going great guns on my chairs.

Jaxxlyn doesn't understand why the raccoon won't drink her water. She asks if I've moved it each day. Then she talks to the raccoon from the porch, talks to him so he pauses in his jaunty walk and looks our way. She alternates from a low, cooing voice to a high, baby voice. The raccoon and I exchange looks. He knows, I think to myself. He knows. He can hardly cart things off as fast as I can steal them back. He knows.

For the next week I am a maker of chairs in the daytime and a sitter of chairs at night. I'm a happy man. Only during the in-between hours do I venture through the woods to the raccoon's house and then venture back in the near-dark. I've taken to putting my booty back in the trash can.

My West Hartford lady drives cross-state to see how her chairs are coming along. I let her run her wealthy fingers across the soft wood, up and down the smooth legs. She shivers and says it feels alive still. "Doesn't it feel alive still?" she says.

Back in the woods I take a different route to the raccoon's tree. I figure I might catch him out this time, but it turns out we've merely switched paths, and he's trying to catch me out. I round the pond quickly, the last fall leaves floating like toy boats on the water, and hurry to the bushes where the crotched branch is hidden. The trees are quiet. I throw the crotch up against the treetrunk, climb quickly up, and in the half-light see that the raccoon has taken the ballpoint pen back.

Still writing sonnets, raccoon? I say and I reach in and take the pen back. But just as I do the den bursts into a flurry of fur and claws and teeth. I hear a hiss, a growling sibilance, and just before I fall see two leathery hands gripped around my wrist and a furry mouth set to bite. An instant later I am lying scratched and hurt in the laurel below. Above me the raccoon peers fiercely down at me from his hole. His eyes are black and fanatical, and he seems to say: "All right? All right? Understand? All right?"

What do you want ? I whisper to the raccoon in my sleep. *What do you want ?*

What do you want ? the raccoon whispers back. *What do you want ?*

On the third night I forsake the chair shop for the junipers, hiding myself long before dusk in the green shrubbery that skirts the forest's edge. It's snowing. The flurries make an icy whisper in the trees overhead. I watch the sun fall through autumn avatars and set in blue winter. The snowflakes land on my eyelashes and melt New England into an antique drizzle. I blink my eyes to clear them and wait with my joints stiffening, my toes disappearing.

By the time the raccoon comes I am iced over, a snowy stump among the evergreens. He pads silently through the snow, leaving tiny handprints behind him on the slushy ground. He doesn't see me. I watch him with frost inside me, my breathing halted, my hands clubbed. He looks for me on the porch, in my rocker, then tries to spy me through my shop window. For an instant he seems stunned by my absence, by the change in things. He turns and peers straight across at where I sit in the frozen junipers. I am certain he sees me, even nod my head at him. For a moment we are poised, balanced, the one against the other. He blinks, acknowledging my presence in the snow, and then with an air of genteel reciprocation, turns and walks straight into the trap.

When I reach him he has his paws on the trap's sides, the fingers outstretched on the fencing. He peers up at me as if to see if I'll take his hands as evidence after all. There are snowflakes on his eyelashes. When I bend over him our breaths mingle in the cold gray New England air.

* * *

*The originating idea for my short story **Hands** came to me in an oddly typical way. Out for a walk along some railroad tracks in Iowa one afternoon, I came across a telephone pole that had a tree growing so near it that when the wind blew, the tree--like some soul out of Dante-- moaned in agony. This struck me at the time as something of a pocket allegory. What it was an allegory for I wasn't completely sure--I'm still not completely sure--but it's from the quick of such thematic moments that I find my stories get their start. In the case of **Hands** the juxtaposition of a moaning tree and a raccoon that steals garbage seemed to resonate with motifs of intrusive civilization on the one hand, and on the other a natural world that was somehow cognizant--perhaps even subversive--of the rage for order that seems to me central to the human mind. It's the exploitation and dramatization of such thematic "riddles" that gives me the biggest kick out of writing fiction. Because, unlike virtually any other intellectual endeavor, in art the riddle must be left unsolved. To solve it, to name in some definitive way what the elements of a story or a poem represent, is to rob the magician of his miracle. It's in the felt correspondences, the telling detail, the power of a story to finally resist the intelligence, that the magic of literature resides.*

Gregory Blake Smith

ABOUT THE AUTHORS

Clare Rossini attended the College of St. Benedict, the Iowa Writer's Workshop, and Columbia University. She has published poems in various small press and university periodicals and has recently completed her first manuscript, tentatively titled *Fish or Angel*. At Carleton, Ms. Rossini teaches courses in American literature and is the director of The Write Place.

Bob Tisdale was born in Caldwell, N.J., attended Princeton, Wesleyan, and Yale Universities, taught at Dartmouth College, and moved to Northfield in 1966. At Carleton he has taught American and African-American literature, modern and contemporary poetry, and expository writing. This year he is teaching creative writing for the first time and wondering why he didn't do so long ago. He has published poems and essays in the *Carleton Miscellany, The Carleton Magazine, The Northfield Magazine*, and has read his work at Carleton and over WCAL.

Mary Moore Easter dances, writes, sings, and combines these acts in original performance and video works. Currently Associate Professor of Dance at Carleton, Easter has presented her work nationally for the last twenty years, receiving a Bush Artists' Fellowship in choreography ('86), a Minnesota Dance Alliance//McKnight choreographer's Award ('88), and an Intermedia Arts Video Grant ('90), among other support. Born in Petersburg Va., she trained first as a musician, with a B.A. from Sarah Lawrence College, graduate study at the Eastman School of Music, an M.A. in Music for Dancers from Goddard College, and music study in Paris with Nadia Boulanger. Her dance study includes work with major dance artists in many technical styles and philosophies.

Born in Furth, West Germany, **Sigi Leonhard** studied at the university of Bonn between 1973 and 1975, followed by a year at the University of Nantes, France, during which she completed a Licence es Lettres Modernes et Philosophie. She later enrolled in the Ph. D. program at Stanford where she received her M.A. in 1978 and her Ph.D. in 1982. Her published work includes articles on Goethe, Christa Wolf and East German film. Poetry and stories have appeared in two anthologies, *Absorb the Colors* and *A Rich Salt Place,* as well as in *Rag Mag.*

Although he has gladly taught at Carleton since 1954, **Wayne Carver** finds his way back whenever he can to Plain City, Utah, where he was born and raised. After doing three years in the Combat Engineers in W.W. II, he graduated from Kenyon College in 1950. He has published fiction and essays. Proudest time: being associate editor and then editor of *The Carleton Miscellany*, 1960-1977. Angriest moment: 1980, when the College trashed it.

Born in Brooklyn, New York, **Susan Jaret McKinstry** has been working her way westward for some time. She received her B.A. and M.A. at Miami University of Ohio, and her Ph.D. at the University of Michigan in contemporary literary theory, history of the novel, modernism, and women writers. She has published articles on T.S. Eliot, Margaret Atwood, Emily Dickinson, Emily Bronte, Jane Austen, and Toni Morrison, co-edited a book on Mikhail Bahktin and feminism, and has begun to combine her curiosity about words and images with her love of theory (particularly feminist and pyschoanalytic) by writing about film and video as art, as critical interpretation, and as cultural meaning.

140

Like Susan Jaret McKinstry, **Keith Harrison** has for many years been moving westward, but from a different point of origin: from Melbourne, Australia, to London, Toronto and Minnesota, where for almost twenty years he has lived in a farm-house on the College arboretum. He has published four main collections of poetry including *The Basho Poems* and, most recently, *A Burning of Applewood*, as well as a translation from the Middle English poem *Sir Gawain and the Green Knight,* published by **The Folio Society** of London. At Carleton he specializes in the teaching of writing and modern poetry.

Jane McDonnell was born in Richmond, Virginia, and grew up near Washington, D.C. Educated at Bryn Mawr, University of North Carolina (Chapel Hill) and Washington University St. Louis, she has taught at Carleton since 1970, where she founded the Women's Studies Program. The passage we print here is from a work in progress tentatively titled *News from the Border*: *an Autistic Boy and His Family*. A piece on mothering autistic children will appear shortly in *Narrating Mothers* (University of Tennessee Press). She has published essays in *Novel, Genre* and *The Carleton Miscellany*.

Gregory Blake Smith is a graduate of Bowdoin College and the Iowa Writers' Workshop. He has published short stories in various literary reviews and is the author of a novel, *The Devil in the Dooryard* (New York: William Morrow and Co., 1986). At Carleton he teaches fiction workshops and American literature. He is currently working on a new novel, *The Last Shakeress*.